Contents

(handwritten in left margin: 20 25 (Hff) Walch 1-7-99)

Acknowledgments

A special thank-you goes to Jerry Winger, the development coordinator, and to Rita Hart. Both were busy with other projects but took time to help me out. I am in their debt.

Thanks to the Jones County Courthouse and the numerous businesses that offered assistance and information: Allied Insurance Co., Brad Deery Motors, Casey's General Stores, Child Development Corp., Clinton County Extension Service, Fareway Food Stores, First Trust and Savings Bank, H&R Block, Iowa Mutual Insurance Co., Jackson County Courthouse, New Horizons Farm Service, Nissen-Caven Realty, Pekin Insurance Co., ReMax Realty, Podaski Insurance, Sherri's Tax Service, and Tri-County Bank & Trust. Without their input, I could never have put the book together.

Thank you to Gary Mohl, my former principal, the first person who encouraged me to pursue publication; his school was also the first to test this program. Thank you to Kirk Snyder, a Midland math teacher, for providing me with feedback while the trial was being run.

The following students deserve special recognition: Melanie Wilson took charge of organizing this project the first year we ran it, and Laura Leinen assisted her. Aaron Horman helped with computer projects for the book, with proofreading, and with various other tasks.

Finally, thank you to my family for their patience, support, help, and encouragement. Whenever I became overwhelmed with the project they provided the push I needed to keep going. I apologize to anyone I may have forgotten to thank or acknowledge.

Cynthia Westphal

Welcome to Big Bucks, Iowa. You and your students are about to embark on a unique educational experience unlike any you may have had before. *Teaching Consumer Concepts* is real life in simulation: Your classroom is the fictional town of Big Bucks, Iowa, whose major employer is Budget Plus Development Corporation. You are Budget Plus's chief executive officer, and your students are your employees, working for various local divisions of the firm. In the process, they learn (1) how to find a job, (2) how to perform on the job, and (3) how to manage their personal finances as they use the income they earn to support themselves and their imaginary family.

GOALS AND OBJECTIVES

Students often enter the world of work ill-prepared to handle many of the financial aspects of independent living. *Teaching Consumer Concepts* was developed to remedy this situation by giving students hands-on preparation in caring for their financial well-being before they leave the security of the classroom.

The primary goals of this course are to teach the basics of making sound financial decisions, to help students learn to use a budget and gain a realistic idea of the current cost of living, and to introduce students to job searching and the benefits of post-secondary education. The simulation encourages active participation and cooperative learning. Students also share in evaluating themselves and their peers.

Major concepts covered include budgeting and living within one's means; preparing cash flow and net worth statements, checks, and deposit tickets; reconciling bank statements; understanding gross versus net pay, loans, and interest; purchasing home insurance; and completing various forms (job applications, income tax, purchase agreements, etc.).

METHODS OF INSTRUCTION

Recommendations follow for how to set up and manage your class. These are recommendations only, so adjust them to suit your particular teaching style.

Traditional Classroom. In a traditional classroom setting, you can use this book as a supplement. Make up four case scenarios (e.g., a single person with one child who works as a Service Station Attendant) and create a budget for each case. Discuss one or two jobs each day. Go through two of the cases as a class, then assign the other two as homework. Let students complete forms, compute bills, and enter information on a cash flow summary as homework. Use the quizzes to check understanding. You could also use quizzes as worksheets.

Nontraditional Classroom. You can determine how much time the simulation takes and how intense it is. We have found that this scenario works well: cover basic concepts of independent living (e.g., cash flow, budgeting) in a traditional classroom during the first semester; explain the jobs during the first two or three weeks of the second semester, still in a traditional setting; then do the budgeting simulation two or three times to finish out the second semester. Most of the commentary assumes that teachers are using this method, although a great deal of the information is valuable for both approaches.

Teacher's Role. The teacher spends most of the class time encouraging students, observing and evaluating their job performance and class participation, giving individual quizzes, and answering questions. Paperwork takes about as much time as for a more traditional class.

ASSESSMENT AND GRADING

The nature of the simulation precludes examining every piece of student work, so we recommend spot-checking. The final grade is determined from quizzes, evaluations by a student auditor and the teacher, class participation, self-evaluations, and a personal packet of information submitted by each student.

The students' general information sheet includes a breakdown of grade percentages for each aspect of this project. You will want to go over these grading requirements with students when you hand out the general information sheet and personal packet materials. In particular, you should stress how many points students earn in the final week or two of the simulation, as this can dramatically affect the final grade. Students must do the preliminary work throughout the project, but they have to do the quiz, cash flow summary, closing net worth statement, income tax forms, bank reconciliations, and self-evaluation in a short period of time at the end of the project. If students don't do the needed work at the beginning or end of the project, they won't have the information required to complete the final personal packet forms. If they don't complete the final personal packet forms, they will lose a lot of their total possible grade points for the simulation. Stress to students that for success, they need to put out consistent effort throughout the project.

TIME REQUIRED

It will take several weeks to do the simulation the first time (with résumés, etc.). Expect to spend at least five to eight weeks if you do everything. The second time you do the simulation, students change jobs and family situations. Although they have to learn a new job, they now have a résumé, cover letter, and job application. They understand how the simulation works and can work through it more efficiently.

A more conservative approach would be to run the simulation only once. If necessary, you can cut the time required for the simulation by assigning jobs rather than having students apply for them. You can also save time by making some expenses (such as food and clothing) a flat percentage of take-home pay, thus eliminating two jobs: Department Store Manager and Grocery Store Manager. Eliminating these jobs will allow more people to work on the other jobs and speed up the process. (One source for current statistics on these costs for your state is your local Cooperative Extension Service.)

Each day's activities on this simulation will take up a full 45- to 50-minute class period, which allows time for explanations of particular aspects of the simulation, setup, student activities, and wrap-up. We have not run the simulation with block scheduling, but the simulation would most likely take up about two thirds of a block-scheduling period. You could fill in the rest of the time with discussion, further explanations, quizzes, or similar activities.

MATERIALS NEEDED

You will need the following items for each student:

- 1" or 2" three-ring binder to hold job information, forms required for completing the job, business record-keeping, commission statements, etc.
- ½" three-ring binder to contain student's personal packet material (cash flow summary, net worth statement, banking and application forms, etc.)
- Dividers for binders
- Calculator
- Two-pocket folders with three-hole punch to file bank information and statements; use a different folder color for each type of account (personal checking, personal savings, business checking) or a single folder with separate envelopes for each type of account

You will also need the following:

- Stapler(s)
- Three-hole punch to insert materials in binder
- Glue sticks (4)
- Department store catalogs (one Spring/Summer, one Fall/Winter, one Christmas, one with appliances); sale ads and flyers (Department Store Manager)
- State tax withholding tables from your state (Payroll clerk)
- Federal tax withholding tables from the IRS (can be obtained by calling 1-800-TAX-FORM or at the IRS Internet Web site: www.irs. ustreas.gov) (Payroll Clerk)
- Federal income tax tables from the IRS (access as noted above) (Payroll Clerk)
- File box to hold bank account file folders (Bank Account Manager)
- Stick-on labels for bank account folders (Bank Account Manager)
- Business envelopes for handing out completed bank statements (Bank Account Manager)
- Small letter organizer—keep extra copies of deposit slips and checks here for students to use as needed (Bank Account Manager)
- Small "check" file box as a bank drop box where students can drop their deposits (Bank Account Manager)
- Pair of dice

  Note: To extend the simulation, have students whose jobs require tax tables, withholding tables, and department store flyers gather those materials themselves

You may also wish to have these optional supplies on hand:

- Thank-you cards for guest speakers
- Pre-inked stamps: "Paid," "Approved," "Cancelled," "Confidential;" students appreciate the realism these add to the project
- Desktop calculator(s) with tape
- Clipboards
- Zipper bags for each student; can hold pens, pencils, calculator, etc.
- Baby name book

Substitute Materials

Teaching Consumer Concepts is a self-contained unit—with the exception of federal and state withholding tables and federal tax tables, it includes all the paperwork you need to operate the course. But feel free to make it more relevant to your particular location by substituting materials that have counterparts in your community and are accessible. For example, you might use actual real estate ads from your local newspaper or—even better—local Multiple Listing Service (MLS) pages from a real estate agent (MLS listings are much more detailed than newspaper ads). You could ask the real estate agent for real estate purchase or leasing agreements as well, and ask a local lender for loan application forms and a local car dealer for motor vehicle purchase agreements. You may also wish to work with actual federal income tax forms, available from the Internal Revenue Service (IRS). (Copies of Form 1040A are supplied with the simulation).

Have your students help you gather these items and any others you decide to use. Remember that if you make any substitutions, you may need to develop your own answer key to check students' work on these forms.

Guest Speakers

To help meet the goals of this curriculum, you might also want to invite members of the community who have expertise in the topics under study to speak to the class about relevant issues. A real estate agent, for example, could give students invaluable tips on what to look for when choosing a home and which financing arrangements make sense. Try to find a professional who is interested in working with the class on a regular basis for the duration of the course. As the unit progresses, students are sure to have questions or problems. The ongoing input of an experienced professional could be an invaluable resource for information and problem solving. You will find specific guest speaker suggestions in the section of this teacher guide titled "Enrichment and Extension Suggestions."

STUDENT JOB ASSIGNMENT BINDERS

Each student needs a complete packet of material relating to his or her job. If you want, you can give all students copies of the material relating to all jobs in the simulation. Giving each student all the material has several advantages. Students can read everything to decide which job or jobs they want to apply for. If they suspect that an error was made on a bill or another form, they can refer to information in the packet to check the work. And, because all students receive the same material, you don't need to make up different packets for different students. The disadvantages of this approach are the increased photocopying and the risk of intimidating some students with a large packet of material.

To perform their own jobs, two students, the Auditor and the Personnel Manager, need copies of everything given to other students, including job descriptions, forms, etc. It is also helpful to have one or two complete packets on hand as a reference for students.

These are the forms, handouts, and other materials to be included in each job packet. (Include one copy of each form and arrange for students to make any additional copies they need in the school office.)

Auditor

> Job description pages
>
> Employee evaluation form (1 per student)
>
> "Confidential" preinked stamp (optional)

Bank Account Manager

> Job description pages
>
> Account description and signature card (3 cards per student)
>
> IRS 1099 statement (1 per student)
>
> Check register/ledger (1 per student, 1 per business)
>
> Personal savings passbook (1 per student)

Checks (15 checks per student, 10 per business)

Savings withdrawal/deposit ticket (3 per student)

Checking deposit ticket (4 per student, 10 per business)

Checking account statement (1 per student, 1 per business)

Checking account reconciliation (1 per student, 1 per business)

Savings account statement (1 per student)

Savings account reconciliation (1 per student)

Two-pocket folders to file bank accounts

File box to hold bank account file folders

Stick-on labels for bank account folders

Business envelopes to hand out completed bank statements

"Cancelled" pre-inked stamp (optional)

Car Dealer

Job description pages

Motor vehicle purchase agreement (1 per student)

Damage and odometer disclosure statements (1 per student)

Car listings (2 copies)

Accounts receivable card (1 per student; in teacher section)

Commission statement (as needed; in teacher section)

"Paid" pre-inked stamp (optional)

Child Care Worker

Job description pages

Registration form (1 per child in day care)

Daily planner (5)

Bubba Bear Day Care bill (1 per student as needed)

Accounts receivable card (as needed; in teacher section)

"Paid" pre-inked stamp (optional)

County Treasurer

Job description pages

Car registration bill (1 per student)

Real estate tax bill (1 per student as needed)

Accounts receivable card (1 per student and 1 per home owner[s]; in teacher section)

"Paid" pre-inked stamp (optional)

Department Store Manager

Job description pages

Department store invoice (1 per student)

Credit card application (1 per student)

Credit card statement (1 per student as needed)

Accounts receivable card (as needed; in teacher section)

Commission statement (as needed; in teacher section)

Department store catalogs (one each: Spring/Summer, Fall/Winter, Christmas, appliances)

"Paid" pre-inked stamp (optional)

Grocery Store Manager

Job description pages

Billing statement (1 per student)

Accounts receivable card (as needed; in teacher section)

"Paid" pre-inked stamp (optional)

Housing Coordinator

Job description pages

Real Estate Agent

House listings (2 copies)

Real estate purchase agreement (as needed)

Financing worksheet (as needed)

Just 4 You Realty statement of account (as needed)

Leasing Agent

Apartment rental listings (2 copies)

Apartment lease agreement (as needed)

Deposit summary/ receipt (as needed)

Accounts receivable card (as needed; in teacher section)

Commission statement (as needed; in teacher section)

Insurance Agent—Home

Job description pages

Home owner/renter insurance application (1 per student)

Accounts receivable card (as needed; in teacher section)

Commission statement (as needed; in teacher section)

"Paid" pre-inked stamp (optional)

Loan Officer

Job description pages

Car loan application (1 per student)

Bank authorization form (1 per student)

Real estate loan application (as needed)

"Approved" pre-inked stamp (optional)

Payroll Clerk

Job description pages

Federal income tax withholding tables (from IRS)

State income tax withholding table (from state)

Payroll worksheet (1 sheet per student)

Statement of earnings and deductions (2 per student)

Payroll check (2 per student)

IRS W-2 form (1 per student)

Personnel Manager

Job description pages

Application for employment (1 per student)

Rejection letter (as needed)

Employee data sheet (1 per student)

IRS W-4 from (1 per student)

Class participation record (1 per student)

Summary of days missed (1 or 2 total)

"Confidential" pre-inked stamp (optional)

Service Station Attendant

Job description pages

Annual mileage worksheet (1 per student)

Monthly statement (1 per student)

Accounts receivable card (1 per student; in teacher material)

"Paid" pre-inked stamp (optional)

Utilities Manager

Job description pages

Phone use slips

Monthly statement (1 per household)

Accounts receivable card (1 per household)

"Paid" pre-inked stamp (optional)

PERSONAL PACKET BINDERS AND STUDENT INFORMATION

Students also need a binder for personal packets. During the course of the simulation, they will add material to this packet, including job application cover letters, résumés, utility bills, and bank account statements. When you distribute the binders at the beginning of the simulation, each one should include a cash flow summary, a net worth statement, and a self-evaluation form. Along with the personal packet forms, you will also give each student a copy of the general information sheet (which includes grading information), the personal financial information pages, and the personal packet chart, information, and forms.

STORAGE AREA

If possible, have space in the classroom for students to store their simulation materials. Each student could have a file box or a mailbox to hold materials and supplies. Make sure the container is large enough to hold both three-ring binders and additional odds and ends.

JOB ASSIGNMENTS

The jobs that students can apply for depend on the number and mix of students in each class. In a large class, have each student apply for a different job and assign more than one student to some jobs. For example, two or more students could be bank account managers and department store managers. In a small class, one person may have to handle more than one job to make sure that enough students are available to cover the time-consuming jobs.

The chart on the next page will help you decide how to combine jobs or double-team individual jobs. The chart shows how the jobs compare on the basis of difficulty, time required to complete the job, and busiest time for the job. For example, you could assign more than one student to jobs that are rated 4 or 5 on the chart. You could assign more than one job rated 1 or 2 to a single student. Or students could double up on easier jobs so a single individual could concentrate on one hard job. One experience running the simulation will give you a much better idea of the mechanics of selecting jobs and what might work best for a particular class.

Some jobs, as indicated on the chart, do not require a lot of time or expertise. You can assign this type of job to lower-ability students, making them integral to the overall success of the simulation. If you have no very low-level students, you might combine an easy and a more challenging job, or two easy jobs.

Some jobs keep students extremely busy for the first two weeks and leave them no time for conducting personal business. After that, their jobs may be essentially over, and they can catch up on their personal packets. Other students may not be swamped by their jobs until later, so they need to handle as much as possible of their personal finances right at the start. When combining jobs, try to choose jobs that peak at different times.

When combining jobs you must determine how to pay the employee. For a student with two salaried positions you could pay either the higher salary or the average of the two (assuming about half time in each position). If you are combining a salaried and a commission job, you might pay the total commission earned plus half the normal salary for the salaried job. If combining two commissioned positions, you could pay half the combined salaries and all of the commissions earned.

For larger classes, some jobs can easily be divided into two jobs. For example, the Housing Coordinator position could be set up as a Real Estate Salesperson and a Leasing Agent.

Job Difficulty and Work Flow

Job Description	Difficulty*	Time Required	Busy Time
Auditor	5	5	steady
Bank Account Manager	4	5	steady
Car Dealer	3	3	early
Child Care Worker	1	1	early
County Treasurer	2	2	middle
Department Store Manager	2	5	steady
Grocery Store Manager	1	2	steady
Housing Coordinator	4	4	early
Insurance Agent—Home	3	3	middle/end
Loan Officer	3	4	early/middle
Payroll Clerk	3	4	steady
Personnel Manager	3	5	steady
Service Station Attendant	2	2	middle
Utilities Manager	3	2	middle

*Rating scale: 1 is easiest; 5 is hardest.

GETTING STARTED

Day 1

Introduce the project. To introduce the simulation, distribute the General Information sheet (page 16) and an employee data sheet for each student (in the Personnel Manager's packet). Go over the introductory information with students. Explain the goals of the project and what is expected of students. Discuss the grading percentages and the need for students to work consistently, as explained in the "Assessment and Grading" discussion earlier in this teacher material.

Determine marital status. A good mix is one third of the students married, one third single, and one third divorced. To determine marital status, use two hats, one for boys and one for girls (to make sure there will be a "husband" for each "wife"). Prepare slips of paper that say "single," "divorced," or "married." Unless couples are to choose their own partners, the "married" slips should also have a number on them—for example, Couple 1, Couple 2, and so on. Students who draw a "married" slip then need to find the person with the matching number.

Determine number of dependent children. An easy way to do this is by rolling a die. A roll of 1, 2, or 3 indicates the number of children in the household. A roll of 4, 5, or 6 indicates that there are no children in the household. Only one partner of a married couple should roll the die. Single and divorced students also roll the die. (A discussion of current statistics on families headed by a single parent is a natural extension here.) If you have a baby name book, students enjoy picking out names for their "children." If parents have one child, it is an infant; two children, an infant and a three-year-old; three children, an infant, a two- or three-year-old, and a five- or six-year-old.

Determine miles driven to work. This can also be done by rolling dice. Students roll both dice, then multiply the number on one die by the number on the other. This gives a range of 1 to 36 miles.

Complete the employee data sheet. Have students fill in an employee data sheet. On it, they should record the information about spouses, children, and miles driven to work.

Day 2

Introduce jobs. Before students apply for or are assigned jobs, discuss what the different jobs involve. Distribute the Job Openings information (pages 17–19). Show how to complete some of the paperwork for each job and how to enter the bill on a cash flow summary. This is also a good time to invite a human resources director as a guest speaker.

Day 3

Describe the application process and begin interviewing. Once students have decided which job(s) to apply for, they should complete a cover letter, a résumé, and a job application form. Hire the Personnel Manager first, to help with job interviews. You could also ask local businesspeople to conduct interviews, which gives students valuable experience interviewing with a stranger.

Day 4

Continue interviewing and follow-up. After interviewing, the applicant should receive a job offer or a rejection letter from the Personnel Manager. When students are offered jobs, give them the appropriate job packet. Help students who receive rejection letters determine their next two career choices, and consider them when you fill these positions. Continue the application and interview process until all students have a job.

Day 5

Distribute and discuss student financial information and personal packets (pages 19–27). Go through each section of these materials to make sure that students understand what is required. Discuss each task that students must complete. Review the grading requirements (from the background information sheet).

Explain the entertainment, miscellaneous, and medical expenses chart. The top of the chart lists entertainment costs for each month according to family size. Explain that each single person and married couple will choose the expense that corresponds to their family size for each month and enter it on their cash flow summary.

In the bottom of the chart are miscellaneous expenses, again according to family size, for each quarter of a year (spring, summer, fall, winter). Each single person and married couple must choose the expense that corresponds to their family size for each quarter and enter it on their cash flow summary.

At the bottom of the chart are medical expenses, according to family size, arbitrarily occurring in selected months. Each single person and married couple must choose the expense that corresponds to their family size for each listed month and enter it on their cash flow summary.

If you do the simulation more than once, have students roll the die for each subsequent simulation. Then have them add the number on the die to, or subtract the number on the die from, each monthly entertainment cost on this chart. For their quarterly miscellaneous expenses, students should multiply the number on the die by 10 before adding it to, or subtracting it from, each expense.

Day 6

Begin the simulation. Students decide for themselves what they need to do and whom they need to see. Use the first 5 or 10 minutes of each class for instructing students on the activities of the day. This might include explaining how forms, such as the cash flow summary, are completed; reminding students of coming deadlines; discussing how to select car insurance; or announcing any business closures for the day. (Occasionally, if students are swamped with work, they can close their office for a day to catch up with business paperwork and organize their personal finances.)

During the remainder of the class, employees meet with one another by appointment or on a drop-in basis. As the CEO of Budget Plus, you also purchase goods and services, and in the process evaluate students' progress in the course.

DAILY AND WEEKLY ROUTINES

Daily Planning

In order to fulfill their job duties and also find time to conduct their personal business, students need to plan each day's activities in advance. To help them budget their time, post two daily appointments forms (page 9) in the classroom for students to fill out. (One form is for the current day, and the other is for the following day. You will need to fill in the day of the week at the top of each form, and you will also need to fill in the "Time period" column with the time your class is actually in session broken down into five-minute increments. You or students can fill in the name[s] of the students who hold each listed job in the parentheses under each job title.)

Students can use the appointments form to schedule meetings with other employees and to schedule time for personal affairs. For example, Tom could put his name down for a 15-minute appointment with the car dealer the next day in order to buy a car. He would also put a large X and "meeting with car dealer" through that time period under his own name and job so that everyone else would know that he will not be available then. Or Tom could X out a block of time on the current day and write in "closed—doing book work." By using the appointments forms, students can be sure to budget their time as needed and remember to attend scheduled meetings. You can check the appointments forms to be sure students are balancing their time demands appropriately and doing what they are supposed to be doing on a given day. The Personnel Manager could use the appointments forms as a reference point when evaluating individual students' class participation.

Enrichment and Extension Suggestions

Ideally, the class should spend four days a week on the simulation and on the fifth day have a guest speaker. A good strategy would be to invite guest speakers whose real-life jobs correspond to each position in the corporate town of Big Bucks. Other guest speakers might include a marriage counselor to discuss the importance of an agreed-upon financial plan to a successful marriage, a hospital administrator to discuss the rising cost of health care, an automobile insurance agent, and an insurance claims adjuster to explain how to file a claim. Suggestions related to specific simulation jobs are given below.

Auditor/Personnel Manager

It works well to have the auditor and personnel manager work together as a team to do the employee training and evaluations. A human resources director as a guest speaker could give information on what employers look for from job applicants, how to conduct an interview and succeed as an interviewee, and effective strategies for training and evaluating employees.

Bank Account Manager

A banking officer as guest speaker could tell students about the many different types of bank accounts available, and related fees, and discuss which type of accounts different types of customers might select. The teacher or a banking officer or an accountant could walk students through the process of reconciling a typical monthly bank statement.

Housing Coordinator

A real estate agent as guest speaker could explain the terms and conditions of paragraph 6 in the real estate purchase agreement, as well as other aspects of buying and leasing property. Students would probably be interested to see a multiple listing book. Local real estate firms might have Web sites with current listings and photos. Relating to the apartment lease, you could use an opening 10-minute class discussion to talk about what "heated," "utilities included," and similar terms mean in apartment rental ads in your local area.

Daily Appointments

Day: _____

Time Period	Auditor	Bank Account Manager	Car Dealer	Child Care Worker	County Treasurer	Depart-ment Store Manager	Grocery Store Manager	Housing Coordi-nator	Insurance Agent—Home	Loan Officer	Payroll Clerk	Personnel Manager	Service Station Attendant	Utilities Manager
	( )	( )	( )	( )	( )	( )	( )	( )	( )	( )	( )	( )	( )	( )

Teaching Consumer Concepts

Insurance Agent—Home

An insurance agent as guest speaker could go into more detail about replacement cost endorsements. There are two types—Type 1 covers personal property; it is very common and is now automatically included on some but not all policies. Type 2 provides replacement cost coverage on the dwelling itself assuming the dwelling was insured properly to begin with (payment amounts larger than the face amount are possible if it would cost more than the face amount to replace the structure); this type of coverage is not as common.

Loan Officer

The teacher or a guest speaker could go over the process of applying for a Stafford student loan, which most students will need if they pursue post-secondary education. The teacher could also devote a class period to the process of amortizing a loan. Students can work out amortization with calculators or with a computer spreadsheet program. If loans in the simulation are amortized, students could use the year-end results on their final net worth statements.

Personnel Manager

The teacher could go over actual W-4 forms and worksheets in class so students can learn how itemizing deductions and having a higher income can affect withholding allowances. A health insurance company representative as guest speaker could discuss different types of coverage and health insurance plans, and could explain the details of deductibles and co-insurance and demonstrate their impact with specific scenarios.

Spot Checks

It is impossible to check every piece of paper produced during the course of this project. Spot-checking is a good way to be sure that students stay on track. You spot-check each employee's work when you make your own purchases (the oral/working quiz). In addition, spot-check two or three customer accounts from each business after the student auditor has audited them so you can also evaluate the auditor's performance. Other evaluation strategies are objective written quizzes, subjective evaluations of class participation, and students' self-evaluations.

Examine students' three-ring binders several times during the project to see if students are keeping up and to check off completed forms. (Collecting a few binders a day, chosen at random, will give you a head start on checking all of the packets at the end of the project.)

Final Check

When the project is completed, check that all forms are filled out and submitted in the appropriate order. Check that amounts on bills match amounts on the cash flow summary. Check the bank reconciliation and net worth statement. Spot-check any other details that concern you.

Federal Tax Filings

One of the students' final tasks in the simulation is to complete a federal income tax return (married couples file joint returns). For the purposes of this project, everyone will file Form 1040A. However, tell students that in real life home owners would probably file Form 1040—a longer version of 1040A that allows deductions for the interest on mortgage payments and other expenses. Also tell them that childless tax filers can often file Form 1040EZ, which is simpler than Form 1040A. You might want to bring copies of Form 1040EZ to class and show students how to fill out this form as well.

Form 1040A and instructions for completing it are in the Assessments section at the back of this book. Have students fill out the form as a final task before administering the job quizzes. You will need to supply federal tax tables and earned income credit tables available either from your local IRS office or at the IRS Internet Web site, <www.irs.ustreas.gov>.

SUGGESTED TIMELINE

The list of suggested deadlines for completing forms on page 12 is organized by job title. Give students copies of this list, or post a copy in class, and at the beginning of each week point out which activities students should be working on during that week. Students' progress depends on the size and ability of the class, so adjust this schedule week by week as you see fit. (You could highlight the activities from several different weeks on the list to adapt the list to your real class-time progress.) Remember that the first time you run the simulation, you will spend a week introducing the project to the class, so factor that time into the timeline schedule.

At times, students in certain positions will be unable to meet all deadlines. For example, the Personnel Manager and the Bank Account Manager will be very busy serving others during Week 1 and will probably be unable to finish their personal work. However, if they are married, their spouses might handle all or part of the personal finances that week.

Encourage salespeople to complete all commissioned sales as quickly as possible so they can submit commission statements in time to receive payment of their commissions in a second paycheck before the course ends.

ADDITIONAL REPRODUCIBLE PAGES

These reproducible pages are to be copied and given to certain students, as noted below.

Accounts Receivable Card

The following employees need to fill out accounts receivable cards to keep track of their customers' billing and payment records: Car Dealer, Child Care Worker, County Treasurer, Department Store Manager, Grocery Store Manager, Housing Coordinator, Insurance Agents, Loan Officer, Service Station Attendant, and Utilities Manager. Provide each of these employees with an initial accounts receivable card; they can make more copies as needed.

Commission Statement

The Car Dealer, Department Store Manager, Housing Coordinator (Real Estate Agent), and Insurance Agent all earn commissions. They each need an initial copy of the commission statement, which they fill out as needed and submit to the Payroll Clerk for payment of their earned commissions.

Computing Monthly Loan Payments

The Department Store Manager, Housing Coordinator (Real Estate Agent), and Loan Officer will need to calculate monthly loan amounts for their customers who need financing. There are three options for calculating monthly loan payments. Each is explained on the Computing Monthly Loan Payments sheet. Help students who are loaning money to their customers to decide which method to use, and provide them with a copy of the **Monthly Loan Payment Table** as well.

SUGGESTED TIMELINE

When forms must be completed, and by whom (in addition to ongoing daily bookkeeping):

Week 1

Everyone: complete beginning Net Worth Statement.

Bank Account Manager: fill out forms to open back accounts, hand out bank account materials to account holders.

Department Store Manager: take credit card applications, start selling and drawing up invoices.

Housing Coordinator: as you find homes for customers, begin to fill out forms (purchase and lease agreements, financing worksheets, etc.).

Payroll Clerk: complete payroll worksheets; issue first set of paychecks by the end of the week.

Personnel Manager: complete W-4 forms, employee data sheets; start recording class participation and attendance.

Week 2

Auditor: start audits and employee evaluation forms this week.

Car Dealer: complete car purchase agreements, disclosure statements.

Child Care Worker: fill out registration forms, billing forms.

County Treasurer: send out real estate tax and car registration bills, if any sales are complete.

Department Store Manager: continue selling and drawing up invoices.

Housing Coordinator: continue with Week 1 paperwork, fill out deposit summary/receipts.

Insurance Agent—Home: take home owner's/renter's insurance applications.

Loan Officer: take loan applications, complete bank authorization forms.

Personnel Manager: continue recording class participation and attendance.

Service Station Attendant: complete annual mileage worksheets.

Utilities Manager: begin computing monthly statements as households are set up.

Week 3

Auditor: continue audits and employee evaluation forms.

Car Dealer: submit commission statements.

Child Care Worker: draw up daily planners.

County Treasurer: continue to send out real estate tax and car registration bills.

Department Store Manager: finish invoices, issue credit card statements, submit commission statements.

Grocery Store Manager: compute and issue monthly bills.

Housing Coordinator: submit commission statements.

Insurance Agent—Home: finish taking insurance applications; submit commission statements.

Loan Officer: finish taking loan applications and completing bank authorization forms.

Payroll Clerk: issue second payroll checks for salaried employees; issue second payroll checks for commissioned employees as commission statements are turned in.

Personnel Manager: continue recording class participation and attendance.

Service Station Attendant: complete and issue monthly statements.

Utilities Manager: finish computing monthly statements and issue them.

Week 4

All employees: federal tax forms, written quizzes.

Auditor: complete audits and employee evaluation forms.

Bank Account Manager: complete and issue bank statements and 1099 forms.

Payroll Clerk: issue remaining paychecks for commissioned employees; issue W-2 forms.

Personnel Manager: complete recording class participation and attendance.

Week 5

All employees: self-evaluation, cash flow summary, net worth statement, savings and checking account reconciliations.

All employees (optional): new job applications for different jobs in another round of the simulation; interview for new jobs.

Teaching Consumer Concepts

Accounts Receivable Card

Name _____   Acct. # _____

Address _____

Date	Description	Invoice #	Amount Due	Amount Paid	Check #	Balance	For Loans	
							Interest	Principal
				Ending Balance:				

Commission Statement

Date _____

Employee Name _____   SS # _____

Occupation _____   Phone _____

Customer	Description* of Sale	Date of Sale	Purchase Price

TOTALS: _____

COMPUTE COMMISSION EARNED: Commission = sales × commission rate

Commission Rate

1. _____ (sales**) × ___ % = _____
2. _____ (sales**) × ___ % = _____

Total monthly commission earned; _____

*Department Store Manager should enter "required" or "luxury."

**Enter the criteria for each rate—for example, the Car Dealer would enter "up to $50,000 in sales" for commission rate #1, and "over $50,000 in sales" for commission rate #2; the Department Store Manager would enter "required purchases" for commission rate #1, and "luxury purchases" for commission rate #2.

Teaching Consumer Concepts

COMPUTING MONTHLY LOAN PAYMENTS

By Formula

This method works best if you have a graphic calculator or other programmable calculator. Otherwise, the formula can get rather cumbersome to work with.

Monthly Payment $= (P \times i) \div [1 - (1 + i)^{-n}]$

Where P = amount borrowed ("principal")

i = interest rate per payment period

n = total number of payments

Example: Assume that you borrow $5,000 for 5 years at 6% annual (yearly) interest and pay off the loan monthly.

Therefore: $P = \$5,000$; $i = 6\% \div 12$ months
$= .5\%$ interest per month

and $n = 5$ years * 12 payments per year $= 60$ total payments

Monthly Payment

$= (\$5,000 \times .005) \div [1 - (1 + .005)^{-60}]$

$= 25 \div .2586278 = \$96.66$

By Tables

One of the easiest ways to compute a monthly payment is to use a table of values based on the interest rate and the length of the loan. The Monthly Payment Table on page 15 gives you those values.

Monthly Payment $= P \div V$

Where P = the principal (amount borrowed)

V = the value from the table

To determine the value from the table you will need to know the annual interest rate and the total number of payments Because table values have been rounded to the nearest thousandth, you may get a slightly different answer from the answer you would get using a calculator or a computer.

Example: Assume that you borrow $5,000 for 4 years at 6% interest. You will make monthly payments on this loan.

Therefore: $P = \$5,000$; $V = 42.580$ (from table, interest rate = 6%; $12 \times 4 = 48$ total payments)

Monthly Payment
$= \$5,000 \div 42.580 = \$117.43$

Note: The table is set up for monthly payments only.

By Business Calculator or Computer

Follow the instructions in the manual for the calculator or computer program, or ask your teacher for help. (All calculators and programs operate a little differently.)

Teaching Consumer Concepts

Monthly Loan Payment Table

Number of Payments	Annual Percentage Rate (APR)								
	5%	6%	7%	8%	9%	10%	11%	12%	18%
12	11.681	11.619	11.557	11.496	11.435	11.375	11.315	11.255	10.908
24	22.794	22.563	22.335	22.111	21.889	21.671	21.456	21.243	21.03
36	33.366	32.871	32.386	31.912	31.447	30.991	30.545	30.108	27.661
48	43.423	42.580	41.76	40.962	40.185	39.428	38.691	37.974	34.043
60	52.991	51.726	50.502	49.318	48.173	47.065	45.993	44.955	39.38
72	62.093	60.340	58.654	57.035	55.477	53.979	52.537	51.150	43.845
84	70.752	68.453	66.257	64.159	62.154	60.237	58.403	56.648	47.579
96	78.989	76.095	73.348	70.738	68.258	65.901	63.660	61.528	50.702
108	86.826	83.293	79.960	76.812	73.839	71.029	68.372	65.858	53.314
120	94.281	90.073	86.126	82.421	78.942	75.671	72.595	69.701	55.499
132	101.374	96.460	91.877	87.601	83.606	79.873	76.380	73.111	57.326
144	108.121	102.475	97.24	92.383	87.871	83.677	79.773	76.137	58.854
156	114.540	108.140	102.242	96.798	91.770	87.12	82.813	78.823	60.132
168	120.646	113.477	106.906	100.876	95.335	90.236	85.539	81.206	61.201
180	126.455	118.504	111.256	104.641	98.593	93.057	87.982	83.322	62.096
192	131.982	123.238	115.313	108.117	101.573	95.611	90.171	85.199	62.843
204	137.239	127.697	119.096	111.327	104.297	97.923	92.134	86.865	63.469
216	142.241	131.898	122.624	114.291	106.787	100.016	93.892	88.343	63.992
228	146.999	135.854	125.914	117.027	109.064	101.910	95.469	89.655	64.43
240	151.525	139.581	128.983	119.554	111.145	103.625	96.882	90.819	64.796
252	155.832	143.091	131.844	121.888	113.048	105.177	98.148	91.853	65.102
264	159.928	146.397	134.513	124.042	114.788	106.582	99.283	92.770	65.358
276	163.825	149.511	137.001	126.031	116.378	107.854	100.300	93.583	65.572
288	167.533	152.444	139.322	127.868	117.832	109.005	101.212	94.306	65.751
300	171.060	155.207	141.487	129.565	119.162	110.047	102.029	94.947	65.901
312	174.415	157.809	143.505	131.131	120.377	110.991	102.761	95.515	66.026
324	177.608	160.260	145.388	132.577	121.488	111.845	103.418	96.020	66.131
336	180.644	162.569	147.144	133.912	122.504	112.618	104.006	96.468	66.219
348	183.533	164.743	148.781	135.145	123.433	113.317	104.534	96.866	66.292
360	186.282	166.792	150.308	136.283	124.282	113.951	105.006	97.218	66.353

Payment = Principal ÷ Table Value

Teaching Consumer Concepts

Budget Plus Inc.: General Information

For the next few weeks, you will be living and working in the town of Big Bucks, Iowa. Your employer is Budget Plus, Inc. With the money you earn you must pay for housing, transportation, food, clothing, insurance, and other items. The objective of this exercise is to teach you something about being on your own, setting up a budget, and living within your means.

All Budget Plus employees receive health insurance, two sick days per quarter, and five personal leave days per year. New employees also receive a $1,000 shopping allowance. Family health insurance premiums are automatically deducted from paychecks of employees who have dependents. If you miss work more than two days per quarter because of illness, the extra days off will be without pay.

To get started, you will find out if you are married (and to whom), or if you are single or divorced. You will also learn if you have any children (one, two, or three). All of these things are determined at random. (If you have one child, it is an infant; two children, an infant and a three-year-old; three children, an infant, a two- or three-year-old, and a five- or six-year-old.)

Next, you will apply for a job available at Budget Plus. You may be interviewed for that position or for a different one. Once you are hired, you will receive a packet of materials relating to your job: a detailed explanation of how to carry out the duties of your job, plus all the forms you will need to do this. As a Budget Plus employee, you must do your job accurately and professionally, treating customers with patience and courtesy, or you may be laid off. While you are out of work, you will not receive a paycheck.

You will use the money you earn at your job to support yourself and your family (if you have one). You will make decisions on how much to spend on things like housing, food, car expenses, clothing, and insurance based on your income.

Your grade for this project will be determined by your class participation, audits of your job performance, your teacher's evaluation of your work, quizzes, your own self-evaluation, and your completion of items in your personal packet (described later). Here is the percentage of your total grade that each aspect of the project accounts for:

Class participation	10%	Personal Packet items:	
Auditor's evaluation	10%	Forms	15%
Teacher's evaluation	10%	Cash flow summary	15%
Written quiz	15%	Bank reconciliations	10%
Self-evaluation	5%	Income tax forms	5%
		New worth statement	5%

Good Luck!!!

JOB OPENINGS

These jobs are currently available at Budget Plus, Inc. Sometimes one or more jobs may be combined. Your CEO (the chief executive officer of the company) will inform you when this is necessary.

Auditor: Helps train employees, audits (checks) each employee's business and personal records at least once during the simulation, checks to see that recommended changes and corrections have been made, and, if necessary, recommends layoffs.
Salary: $37,000   *Post-secondary education:* 4 years

Bank Account Manager: Helps employees open checking and savings accounts; checks accuracy of deposit and withdrawal slips; posts checks, deposits, and withdrawals to the appropriate account; prepares bank statements; helps customers reconcile their accounts, if necessary; completes end-of-year 1099 forms.
Salary: $18,600   *Post-secondary education:* 1 year

Car Dealer: Helps customers find a suitable new or used vehicle; fills out purchase agreements, odometer disclosure statements, and physical damage disclosure statements; collects down payment at time of sale and final payment after financing has been arranged.
Salary: $10,000 plus commissions   *Additional Benefit:* Use of
of 1% of total sales up to $50,000   company car
and 2% of total sales over $50,000   *Post-secondary education:* 2 years

Child Care Worker: Determines costs for child care on the basis of current day care rates; plans daily activities for children in day care; keeps current records on each child enrolled in day care.
Salary: $15,000 plus free child
care for worker's own children   *Post-secondary education:* none

County Treasurer: Computes bills and collects payments for automobile registrations; computes annual real estate taxes.
Salary: $28,000   *Post-secondary education:* 4 years

Department Store Manager: Uses catalogs and sale flyers to help customers purchase clothing, furniture, appliances, and other items; conducts cash and credit sales transactions.

Salary: $15,000 plus commissions
of 5% of total sales of necessities
(needs) and 10% of total sales of
luxuries (wants)   *Post-secondary education:* 4 years

Grocery Store Manager: Determines monthly food bill for customers on the basis of family size and personal tastes.

Salary: $24,000   *Post-secondary education:* 4 years

Housing Coordinator: Serves both as real estate agent and as leasing agent. Real estate agent finds homes for people; fills out purchase agreements; collects deposits and down payments; helps arrange financing and evaluate alternatives; and collects closing costs and final payments. Leasing agent helps clients find suitable rental housing; fills out lease and security agreements; collects rent and key and security deposits.

Salary: $10,000 plus commission
of 6% of real estate sales   *Post-secondary education:* 3 years

Insurance Agent: Fills out application and binder forms for insurance on homes and apartments; explains coverage to clients.

Salary: $18,000 plus commissions
of 20% on home owner's or
renter's insurance sold   *Post-secondary education:* 2 years

Loan Officer: Helps arrange for car and home loans; fills out paperwork for each loan that meets financial guidelines; computes and collects monthly payments.

Salary: $26,000   *Post-secondary education:* 4 years

Payroll Clerk: For each semimonthly pay period, computes gross salary, commission, and amounts withheld for federal tax, state tax, Social Security (FICA), Medicare, and family health insurance premiums to determine net pay for each employee; issues payroll checks; completes end-of-year W-2 forms.

Salary: $19,600   *Post-secondary education:* 1 year

Personnel Manager: Helps hire and train employees; reviews employee data sheets and W-4 worksheets; keeps attendance records; evaluates job performance based on active participation.

Salary: $37,000   *Post-secondary education:* 4 years

Service Station Attendant: Computes car expenses for each employee (gas, oil changes, tires, and tune-ups based on annual mileage).
Salary: $18,000   *Post-secondary education:* 1 year

Utilities Manager: Bills customers for gas, electricity, sewer, water, and phone use on the basis of house/apartment size and family size.
Salary: $28,000   *Post-secondary education:* 4 years

PERSONAL FINANCES

Start-up Cash Available

You have the following financial resources to draw on as the simulation begins.

- Personal checking account—$400 (married couples can set up two individual accounts with $200 in each, or one joint account with $400).
- Savings account—20% of annual gross pay (commissioned employees should assume a gross pay of $24,000).
- Cash value of old life insurance policy: 20% of gross pay (commissioned employees should assume a gross pay of $24,000). This is an old policy that your parents bought when you were a baby. It has built up a cash value that you can borrow against to make down payments on a house or car. It is like borrowing your own money. You have to pay it back, but you can borrow at a low interest rate. (In real life, the insurance company would take the interest payment out of the amount you borrow, so the amount you actually had to use would be the loan amount minus the interest payment. In this simulation, you simply borrow up to the full cash value of your insurance policy and make no interest payment during the simulation.)
- Business checking account—check with the Bank Account Manager to find out the beginning balance of your business account.

You pay a checking service charge of $5.00 per month on both your personal and business checking accounts.

Other Assets

- Trade-in value of your existing car—$1,500.

Teaching Consumer Concepts

Check Deposits

Once you are employed, you will receive a regular paycheck. You will open bank accounts and deposit your paycheck in them. You'll use the money from your paycheck to pay your expenses.

Checks must be endorsed before they can be deposited. Endorse them by signing them on the back with the same name that the check is made out to. **Endorse checks as soon as you receive them.** Use restricted endorsements—they are safer. A restricted endorsement uses the words "For deposit only to the account of . . . " Here is an example of a restricted endorsement for a payroll check: "For deposit only to the account of Juanita L. Campos." Here is an example of a restricted endorsement for a business check: "For deposit only to the account of Bubba Bear Day Care."

Payroll Checks. Put 5 percent of your net pay into your savings account, using a savings deposit slip. Put the rest of your net pay into your checking account, using a checking deposit slip. (See the sample paycheck and deposit slips below. You will receive these forms from the Bank Account Manager when you open your checking and savings accounts.) **Keep track of all personal deposits, withdrawals, and checks in your check register or savings passbook.**

Business Checks. Deposit these checks into your business checking account daily, using a checking deposit slip. Make out a business check payable to Budget Plus for 80 percent of the deposit and give it to the Payroll Clerk. This payment covers the cost of your salary and overhead for your business (electricity, supplies, insurance, and so on). **Keep track of all checks and deposits in your business ledger.**

Budget Plus, Inc.
430 Consumer Lane
Big Bucks, IA 00000

Check No. _____001_____

Date _____4/2/99_____

Pay to the
Order of __Sue B. Smith_____ $ ___875.43___

___eight hundred seventy-five and 43/100_____ **Dollars**

Big Bucks
Savings Bank

_____ Lyle Thomas _____
Budget Plus, Inc., *Payroll Clerk*

⑈071458⑈ 138472⑈ 2428

Checking Deposit Ticket

Name Sue B. Smith
(Personal account)

Business Name _____
(Business account)

Address 1282 Highland
Big Bucks, IA 00000

Account No. _____

Date 4/3/99

_____
sign here for cash received

Big Bucks
Savings Bank

Currency		
Coin		
Checks (list each check separately)		
Budget Plus, Inc.	875	43
Less Savings	43	77
Total	831	66
Less Cash Received		
Net Deposit	831	66

Be sure each item is properly endorsed!

Savings

Withdrawal

Date 4/3 , 19 99

Name Sue B. Smith

Address 1282 Highland
Big Bucks, IA 00000

Account number S-03

Amount withdrawn **$** _____

Sign here _____

Big Bucks
Savings Bank

Deposit

Cash		
Check Description		
From Checking		
Deposit	$43	77
Total Checks	$43	77
Less Cash Received		
Total Deposit	$43	77

EXPENSE PAYMENTS

You will receive a paycheck twice a month. Each time you receive a paycheck, you must use your income to pay your expenses. The chart on the following page lists the schedule for paying expenses. When you use a check to pay a particular expense, make out your check for payment to the business named next to the expense in the chart. For example, when you pay for food, make the check out to "Food Fair." In the case of some expenses, as noted in the chart, you will simply record the expense in your cash flow and will not write out a check for that expense.

Teaching Consumer Concepts

Payment Period	**Expense**
Monthly	Mortgage—Big Bucks Savings Bank
	Rent—Budget Plus Development Corporation
	Utilities—City Utilities, Inc.
	Car loan—Big Bucks Savings Bank*
	Car expense—Gas & Go Service Station
	Food—Food Fair
	Clothing, furniture, etc.—Heart & Home Department Store
	Day care—Bubba Bear Day Care
	Entertainment expense**
Occasional months............	Medical expenses**
Quarterly...........................	Miscellaneous expenses**
Semiannual (March & September)	Real estate taxes—Ward County Treasurer**
Annual	Home owners insurance—Country Insurance Agency
	Renters insurance—Country Insurance Agency
	Car registration—Ward County Treasurer** (due in month of your birth)
	Income tax payable—Internal Revenue Service** (pay in April if owed)
One-time expenses	Down payment and closing costs for real estate***
	Down Payment for car***
	Security deposit on apartment***

*Automatic deduction from checking account. Deduct payment from your check register.

**Enter on cash flow only. Do not write a check for this expense.

***Money can come from savings, cash value of life insurance, or loans. Pay by check but do not include on cash flow.

Teaching Consumer Concepts

Entertainment Costs and Miscellaneous and Medical Expenses

Entertainment Costs

		January	February	March	April	May	June
Activity:		Flea Market	Garage Sale	Party	Ice Capades	Fishing	Weekend Getaway
Family Size:	1	$10	$20	$8	$10	$4	$75
	2	$18	$15	$14	$15	$8	$100
	3	$6	$9	$18	$20	$12	$125
	4	$8	$12	$22	$25	$16	$150
	5	$10	$15	$25	$30	$20	$175

		July	August	September	October	November	December
Activity:		Water Skiing	MiniGolf	Wedding (gift)	Circus	Museum	Football Game
Family Size:	1	$5	$5	$15	$5	$4	$6
	2	$8	$7	$8	$8	$8	$10
	3	$12	$9	$8	$11	$12	$13
	4	$15	$11	$12	$14	$16	$15
	5	$18	$13	$9	$17	$20	$18

Miscellaneous Expenses

		Spring	Summer	Fall	Winter
Expense:		Car Trouble	Job Training	IRS Audit	Dentist
Family Size:	1	$300	$250	$150	$60
	2	$75	$100	$50	$35
	3	$200	$0 (employer pays)	$100	$70
	4	$100	$100	$350	$150
	5	$85	$500	$50	$125

Medical Expenses

		February	April	May	July	October	December
Family Size:	1	$10	$20	$90	$5	$5	$10
	2	$25	$10	$15	$30	$5	$55
	3	$5	$15	$45	$10	$75	$5
	4	$10	$5	$20	$55	$10	$15
	5	$50	$10	$15	$5	$30	$75

PERSONAL PACKET

This packet contains a cash flow summary, net worth statement, and self-evaluation that you must complete as part of this simulation. You will collect a variety of other forms regarding your personal finances, which you must add to your packet. All the forms that your completed personal packet must contain are listed in the charts on the next page.

Teaching Consumer Concepts

Section Title	Form Required	Prerequisite	Contact
General	Cash Flow Summary	paychecks/bills/taxes	Teacher
	Employee Data Sheet(s)	none	Personnel Manager
	Cover Letter(s)	none	Personnel Manager
	Résumé(s)	none	Personnel Manager
	Job Application(s)	none	Personnel Manager
	W-4 Form(s)	job application	Personnel Manager
	Payroll Stubs (2 per person)	W-4 form/commission statements	Payroll Clerk
Car Expenses	Motor Vehicle Purchase Agreement(s)	open checking account	Car Dealer
	Disclosure Statements	auto purchase agreement	Car Dealer
	Car Loan(s)	purchase agreement	Loan Officer
	Gas & Go Bill(s)—Car Expense	auto loan approval	Service Station Attendant
	Car Registration	auto loan approval	County Treasurer
Other Expenses	*Food Fair* Monthly Grocery Bill	open checking account	Grocery Store Manager
	Heart & Home Department Store Bill	open checking account	Department Store Manager
	Bubba Bear Child Registration Form(s)	none	Child Care Worker
	Bubba Bear Day Care Monthly Bill	child registration forms	Child Care Worker
Income Tax Forms	W-2 form(s)— end-of-year summary	second paycheck	Payroll Clerk
	Form 1099 Interest Income	savings account statement	Bank Account Manager
	1040A	W-2, child care, 1098, 1099	Teacher
Banking Forms	Signature Card(s)	none	Bank Account Manager
	Check Register	none	Bank Account Manager
	Checking Account Statement	make deposits, pay bills	Bank Account Manager
	Savings passbook	none	Bank Account Manager
	Savings Account Statement	end of project	Bank Account Manager
Summary Information	Net Worth Statement	cash flow complete	Teacher
	Self-Evaluation	end of project	Teacher

Married couples are required to buy a house. Single or divorced people can buy a house or rent an apartment. Here are the forms your personal packet must include, depending on whether you buy a house or rent an apartment.

© 1998 J. Weston Walch, Publisher

Teaching Consumer Concepts

Section Title	Form Required	Prerequisite	Contact
House Expenses	Real Estate Purchase Agreement	open checking account	Housing Coordinator
	Just 4 You Realty Statement	purchase agreement	Housing Coordinator
	Home Owner's Insurance Application	purchase agreement	Insurance Agent—Home
	Residential Loan Application	purchase agreement and insurance	Loan Officer
	Real Estate Taxes	home loan approval	County Treasurer
	City Utilities, Inc., Bill	home loan approval	Utilities Manager
OR			
Apartment Expenses	*Budget Plus Dev. Corp.—* Apt. lease	open checking account	Housing Coordinator
	Security Deposit Summary/ Receipt	apartment lease	Housing Coordinator
	Renter's Insurance Application	apartment lease	Insurance Agent—Home
	City Utilities, Inc., Bill	apartment lease	Utilities Manager

Keep the page with the charts at the front of your personal packet binder, and use it as a checklist. Organize your personal packet information in the order listed on the charts.(Married couples submit one combined personal packet binder, with two self-evaluation forms.)

Your teacher will check your personal packet binder from time to time during the project, so be sure to keep the binder current. You must turn in your personal packet binder to your teacher at the project's end. Your teacher will use this packet to help determine your grade for the project. The percentage that each item in your personal packet counts toward your final grade is given on the background information sheet for Budget Plus, Inc.

Cash Flow Summary. Keep the cash flow summary handy and complete it as you go. For example, once you have seen the Grocery Store Manager and determined your monthly bill, write out a check to pay for a month's food and record the amount of the check on the check register. Because food is a monthly expense, enter the same amount for all months on the Food line of the cash flow summary. Compute the total spent on food for the year in the totals column.

Net Worth Statement. Fill out the "Start of Project" part on the net worth statement about yourself at the beginning of the simulation. The "Personal Finances" section of your project background information will give you some of the information you need for the net worth statement. You'll acquire other information as you make decisions on homes and car purchases. At the end of the simulation, fill out the "End of Project" portion of the net worth statement. (You can list full loan amounts for the ending figures, or you can list amounts after amortizing.) Compare beginning and ending figures. Have you budgeted and spent wisely and increased your net worth?

Self-Evaluation. At the end of the simulation, you will complete this self-evaluation form. Be objective. Your self-evaluation will count for 5 percent of your project grade.

Teaching Consumer Concepts

Cash Flow Summary for _____

	Jan.	Feb.	March	April	May	June	July	Aug.	Sept.	Oct.	Nov.	Dec.	Total
INCOME													
Net Monthly Pay													
Spouse's Net Pay													
Interest Income													
Income Tax Refund													
TOTAL INCOME:													
EXPENSES													
Mortgage or Rent													
Home or Renter's Insurance													
Utilities–Electric													
Gas													
Water/Sewer													
Garbage													
Phone													
Real Estate Taxes													
Car #1–Loan Payment													
Registration													
Car Expense													
Car #2–Loan Payment													
Registration													
Car Expense													
Food													
Department Store Purchases													
Child Care Expenses													
Entertainment Expenses													
Miscellaneous Expenses													
Medical Expenses													
Gifts													
Church or Charity													
Income Tax Due													
Savings Plan (5%)													
TOTAL EXPENSES:													
GAIN OR LOSS													

Net Worth Statement

Name: _____ **Date:** _____

Assets:	Start of Project	End of Project
Checking account balance	_____	_____
Savings account balance	_____	_____
Cash value of life insurance	_____	_____
Market value of real estate	_____	_____
Cash value of car #1	_____	_____
Cash value of car #2	_____	_____
Other	_____	_____
Total Assets	_____	_____
Liabilities:		
Mortgage balance	_____	_____
Car loan #1	_____	_____
Car loan #2	_____	_____
Other	_____	_____
Total Liabilities	_____	_____
New Worth (Total assets − Total liabilities)	_____	_____

Self-Evaluation

Name: _____ **Date:** _____

Circle the number you feel most accurately reflects your performance during this project.

	Strongly Disagree				Strongly Agree
1. **Conduct:** I performed my job in a professional manner.	1	2	3	4	5
2. **Understanding:** I understood the duties of my job.	1	2	3	4	5
3. **Accuracy:** Forms were filled out neatly and accurately.	1	2	3	4	5
4. **Completeness:** Forms and explanations were complete.	1	2	3	4	5
5. **On-Task:** I kept busy working on the project and did not get sidetracked.	1	2	3	4	5
6. **Budget:** I stayed within my budget and had money left over.	1	2	3	4	5

7. On a separate sheet of paper, explain what you have learned and what grade you feel you have earned on this project (one page minimum). Discuss things that you were proud of and things that you could improve. What are your goals for the next time you do the project? Give any recommendations you have for improving the project.

Teaching Consumer Concepts

Auditor

Job Description: Needs to understand all jobs at Budget Plus, Inc., to train and evaluate other employees. Checks each employee's business and personal records at least once during the simulation, and follows up to determine whether employee has made recommended changes or corrections. Recommends promotions and layoffs.

Educational Requirements: Undergraduate degree in business administration or employee relations (master's degree preferable, but not required).

Benefits: Starting salary—$37,000 with annual reviews. Health insurance coverage provided—individual. Shopping allowance—$1,000 (new employees only). Sick days—two per quarter. Personal Days— five per year.

Duties

Train employees. Make sure each employee knows what her or his job is and how to do it, and how to complete required forms. The auditor's own performance evaluation is based, in part, on how well fellow employees perform their jobs.

Audit employees. Audit each employee at least once during the simulation and complete an Employee Evaluation Form (Form A) for each audited worker. As soon as training is complete and employees feel comfortable in their jobs, usually a few days into the simulation, begin auditing. Complete at least one audit per day.

1. Choose an employee to audit. (Audits are done without advance warning.) Read the job description for the employee you are about to audit.
2. Introduce yourself and tell the employee that you are about to begin an audit. Choose two customer files completed by the employee. Check that all forms are correctly filled out.
   • Name, address, phone number, etc., are correct.
   • Information about the employee's business is correct.
   Example: Auditing the Bank Account Manager. Make sure that checks and deposits are recorded in the right accounts; beginning

balances are correct; daily balances are correct; signature cards are completed, etc.

Example: Auditing the Payroll Clerk. Make sure that W-4 information was transferred correctly; gross pay and commission are correct; health insurance is withheld when appropriate; deductions for income taxes, FICA, and Medicare are computed correctly; and checks are issued on time.

3. Be sure that business bookkeeping records are accurate and up-to-date.
   - Checks have been correctly endorsed and deposited daily.
   - Business checking account balance is current.
   - Records are accurate for accounts receivable.
   - When appropriate, Budget Plus has been reimbursed for 80 percent of all deposits.
4. Be sure that personal records are current.
   - Necessities (food, clothing, shelter) have been secured in a timely manner.
   - Cash flow has been updated as items are purchased.
   - Check register and savings book are accurate and current.
   - Bills have been paid on time.
5. Observe the employee interacting with a client.
   - Is the employee knowledgeable about the job?
   - Does the employee take time to inform the client, for example, does the Housing Coordinator explain why a house purchase includes closing costs?
6. Discuss with the employee any problems you noticed during the audit that need to be corrected.

After a few days, do a follow-up visit to see if the problems you discussed have been corrected. If not, try to find out why. Inform your CEO (teacher) of any problems still unresolved when you made the follow-up visit.

Give the Employee Evaluation Form and the two customer files that you checked to your teacher.

Form A—Auditor/Employee Evaluation form

Employee Evaluation

Employee _____   **Date** _____

Position _____

Please rate the employee on the following attributes. (Rating scale: 5 = excellent, 4 = good, 3 = satisfactory, 2 = poor, 1 = unsatisfactory)

General Information

Uses time well.	1	2	3	4	5
Demonstrates self-control and poise in all areas of the job, such as manners, professionalism, and conduct.	1	2	3	4	5
Works well with colleagues.	1	2	3	4	5
Communicates skillfully.	1	2	3	4	5
Is knowledgeable about job.	1	2	3	4	5
Cooperates fully with auditor.	1	2	3	4	5

Personal Records

Tasks are being completed on time.	1	2	3	4	5
Bills are being paid and checking account is accurate and up-to-date.	1	2	3	4	5
Employee is working on net worth and cash flow summaries.	1	2	3	4	5

Comments: _____

_____

Business Bookkeeping Records

All transactions are recorded in business ledger.	1	2	3	4	5
Checks are endorsed and deposited daily.	1	2	3	4	5
Business checking account is accurate and up-to-date.	1	2	3	4	5
Budget Plus is being reimbursed, if appropriate.	1	2	3	4	5

Comments: _____

_____

_____ *(continued)*

      Teaching Consumer Concepts

Form A—Auditor/Employee Evaluation form (continued)

Business Information

Customer Records Checked:

1. Customer Name _____ Position _____

Forms are filled out completely and neatly.   1   2   3   4   5

Basic information obtained from customer (size of house,
number of children, type of vehicle, address) is correct.   1   2   3   4   5

Computations are accurate.   1   2   3   4   5

Any problems noted and discussed: _____

_____

2. Customer Name _____ Position _____

Forms are filled out completely and neatly.   1   2   3   4   5

Basic information obtained from customer (size of house,
number of children, type of vehicle, address) is correct.   1   2   3   4   5

Computations are accurate.   1   2   3   4   5

Any problems noted and discussed: _____

_____

Follow-up Visit

Recommended changes have been made. _____ yes _____ no

Comments: _____

_____

_____

_____

Points Earned: _____   Points Possible: _____   Percentage Earned: _____

Evaluation: Excellent   Satisfactory   Probationary   Poor

Recommendation: Promotion   No change   Terminate   Grade: _____

Auditor's Signature _____ Date _____

Teacher's Signature _____ Date _____

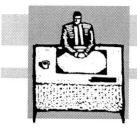

Bank Account Manager

Job Description: Helps bank customers open new accounts, make deposits, withdraw and transfer funds; sorts and files checks and deposits; sends out overdraft notices or returns bad checks; makes up monthly bank statements and helps customers resolve any disagreements over bank statements. Prepares end-of-year interest income statements.

Educational Requirements: High school diploma and a minimum of one year of post-secondary education in business.

Benefits: Starting salary—$18,600 with semiannual reviews. Health insurance coverage provided—individual. Shopping allowance—$1,000 (new employees only). Sick days—two per quarter. Personal days—five per year.

Duties

Open Personal Checking Accounts

1. Complete Account Description and Signature Cards (Form A).
   - Fill out a separate card for each account (personal checking, personal savings, and business checking).
   NOTE: Married couples may have either two separate accounts or one joint account. If they choose separate accounts, the couple must decide who can sign checks: the account holder only or the account holder and the spouse. If the couple chooses a joint account, their names should be listed in one of the following ways: John D. *or* Mary S. Doe, Ryan M. Smith *or* Karen C. Glifford. Explain to clients that using "or" instead of "and" makes things easier for a surviving spouse if something should happen to one of them.
   - Use first name, middle initial, and last name as the valid signature. When employees make out business checks, be sure they write the business's name on the check as well as signing it. Otherwise, the money could be taken out of their personal account. Bank employees compare the signature on the card with the signature on checks to make sure checks are not forged.

2. Assign consecutive account numbers beginning with the letter C (for checking): C-01, C-02, etc.
3. Hand out personal check registers (Form B), personal checks (Form C), and checking deposit slips (Form D) to all clients.
   • Have customers write their name, address, and account number on all checks and deposits.
4. Remind students to enter $400 as the beginning balance on the check register for personal checking account ($200 if married with separate accounts). Advise all customers of the $5.00 monthly service charge deducted automatically from the account.

Open Savings Accounts

1. Fill out Account Description and Signature Cards (Form A), and assign consecutive account numbers beginning with the letter S (for Savings): S-01, S-02, etc.
2. Hand out savings deposit/withdrawal slips (Form E) and savings passbooks (Form F). Tell customers they can pick up more from you when they run out.
3. Remind customers that their beginning savings balance is 20 percent of their annual salary. For married couples, the beginning savings balance is 20 percent of the combined total of both salaries.
   • Check job description sheets to determine annual salary. Assume an annual salary of $24,000 for commissioned jobs.
4. Remind students that they must deposit 5 percent of each paycheck in their savings account and that instructions on making deposits are in the "Check Deposits" section of their student background information.

Open Business Checking Accounts

1. Determine whether the client needs a business account. (See the list of business accounts and starting balances that comes with this job packet.) If two or more people are doing one job that requires a business account, they use the same business ledger and sign the same signature card.
2. Fill out Account Description and Signature Cards (Form A). Assign consecutive account numbers beginning with the letter B (for Business): B-01, B-02, etc., and hand out business checking ledger (Form B), business checks (Form C), and deposit slips (Form D).
3. Inform clients of their beginning balance, and advise them of the $5.00 monthly service charge deducted automatically from the account.

Teaching Consumer Concepts

Post and File Transactions (All Accounts)

1. Check the accuracy of deposits: Watch for addition or subtraction errors and missing endorsements. Make sure that 5 percent of paycheck is being deposited in savings, and that client's name and address appear on both checks and deposit tickets.

2. Set up a folder for each account.
   - Color-code folders—for example, you might make all personal checking folders blue, savings folders red, business accounts green.
   - Put folders in alphabetical order according to the type of account, and in numerical order within each letter—e.g., B-01, B-02, C-01, C-02, S-01, S-02.
   - Put bank statements in the middle of the folder.
   - The front pocket is for outstanding checks and deposits. The back pocket is for all checks and deposits that have been posted to that account.

3. File deposit/withdrawal slips and checks in the appropriate account folder.

4. Post checks and deposits to the appropriate accounts. "Posting" is the bank's method of keeping track of money going into an account (deposits) and money going out (checks or withdrawals). (See sample postings on pp. 38–41.) For example, suppose that client Sue Smith writes a personal check to business Food Fair. When Food Fair deposits the Smith check, you must deduct that amount from Smith's personal checking balance and add it to Food Fair's business checking balance. The transaction must be recorded on both bank statements. The deposit triggers the process, because the Smith check is in Food Fair's possession until Food Fair fills out a deposit slip and deposits it. Only then is the check subtracted from the Smith account. (See p. 41.)
   - Pull each account folder and list each check, withdrawal slip, or deposit slip in the front pocket on the bank statement (Form G). Record each transaction in all accounts that it affects.
   - Stamp each check, withdrawal slip, or deposit slip with a "canceled" stamp once it is recorded. If you don't have a stamp, make a large checkmark on the back of the check or slip.
   - Place canceled checks and withdrawal/deposit slips in the back pocket of the folder.

5. Every week, double-check for filing errors.
   - Pull each account file and look quickly at signatures to make sure no checks are filed in the wrong account.
   - Count the number of canceled checks/withdrawal slips filed in an account and see if it matches the number of checks

Teaching Consumer Concepts

posted to (that is, subtracted from) that account on the bank statement.

- Count the number of canceled deposit slips filed in an account and see if it matches the number of deposits posted to (that is, added to) that account on the bank statement.

Make up Checking Statements (Form G)

1. Record the $5.00 monthly service charge on each checking account statement. Then, compute and record the closing balance.
2. Fold statements, place in envelopes with canceled checks and deposit slips, and deliver to clients.
   NOTE: Usually, not all transactions will be complete when you make up the bank statements. (For example, Food Fair may not have deposited Smith's check yet.) These checks are simply listed as outstanding when the client does his or her bank reconciliation (Form H).
   NOTE: Set up a small file box for students to drop their deposits in.

Make up Savings Account Statements (Form I)

Let "day 1" be the first day of the project (the first day the bank is open for business), "day 2" be the second day, etc. The account balance as of day 1 is the beginning balance. It does not change until the client makes a deposit or withdrawal.

1. Write the daily balances under the balance column for each numbered day. To keep up-to-date, do this daily or each time a deposit or withdrawal is made.
2. At the end of the simulation, or after 31 days, whichever comes first, add up the daily balances and divide by the number of days to determine the average daily balance.
3. Compute the interest earned:
   Interest = principal × rate × time; or $I = p \times r \times t$
   - Let the average daily balance be p.
   - Convert the interest rate to a decimal to use in the formula. This is the r, or rate.
   - The bank pays its customers interest on their accounts monthly. The interest rate is an annual rate that must be divided by 12 to compute a monthly interest payment, so your t value is $\frac{1}{12}$. Multiplying by $\frac{1}{12}$ is the same as dividing by 12. Either change $\frac{1}{12}$ to a decimal and multiply (p × r) by that decimal, *or* divide (p × r) by 12.
   - Compute the current balance by adding the month's interest to the last daily balance.

NOTE: Some transactions may not be complete when you make up this bank statement. (For example, Sue Smith may have made an after-hours deposit in the deposit file box.) These deposits will be listed as outstanding when the client does her or his bank reconciliation (Form J).

Complete the 1099 Interest Income Form

At year end, you must let customers know how much interest they earned on their savings so that they can report this income on their tax return.

1. To compute annual interest earned, multiply one month's interest by 15. This is not completely accurate, but accurate enough for our simulation. Because the interest is compounded (the bank pays its clients interest on the interest that it adds to their accounts each month) and clients continue to deposit 5 percent of each paycheck to their accounts, throughout the year, multiplying by 15 is close enough.

2. Complete the 1099 (Form K), as shown below, and send it to your customers.

9595   ☐ VOID   ☐ CORRECTED

PAYER'S name, street address, city, state, ZIP code, and telephone no. ***Budget Plus, Inc.*** 430 Consumer Lane Big Bucks, IA 00000	1 Rents $	OMB No. 1545-0115 19**98** Form 1099-MISC	Miscellaneous Income
	2 Royalties $		
	3 Other income $		
PAYER'S Federal identification number 14-378931	RECIPIENT'S identification number 120-00-6700	4 Federal income tax withheld $	5 Fishing boat proceeds $	Copy A For **Internal Revenue Service Center**
RECIPIENT'S name Denzel Roe		6 Medical and health care payments $	7 Nonemployee compensation $	File with Form 1096.
Street address (including apt. no.) 1460 County Rd. W-32		8 Substitute payments in lieu of dividends or interest $	9 Payer made direct sales of $5,000 or more of consumer products to a buyer (recipient) for resale ▶ ☐	For Paperwork Reduction Act Notice and instructions for
City, state, and ZIP code Monticello, IA		10 Crop insurance proceeds $	11 State income tax withheld $	completing this form, see **Instructions for Forms 1099, 1098,**
Account number (optional) S-14	2nd TIN Not. ☐	12 State/Payer's state number	13 **Interest Income** $ 351.96	**5498, and W-2G.**

Form **1099-MISC**   48-097 1237   Department of the Treasury - Internal Revenue Service
Do NOT Cut or Separate Forms on This Page

Teaching Consumer Concepts

BEGINNING ACCOUNT BALANCES

Personal Checking Accounts: Each account starts with $400, except for married couples with individual accounts, who split their $400 into $200 apiece.

Personal Saving Accounts: Each account starts with 20 percent of an account holder's annual gross salary. Commissioned employees start with 20 percent of $24,000. Married couples start with 20 percent of their gross combined salaries.

Business Checking Accounts: Account names and balances are listed below.

Big Bucks Savings Bank Loan Account	$1,500,000
Bubba Bear Day Care	500
Budget Plus, Inc.: Payroll Account	750,000
Budget Plus Development Corp.: Rental Account	500
City Utilities, Inc.	500
Colden's Cool Cars	500
Country Insurance Agency	250,000
Food Fair	500
Gas & Go Service Station	500
Heart & Home Department Store	500
Just 4 You Realty	500
Ward County Treasurer	500

Teacher's Account: Open a personal checking account for your teacher as CEO of Budget Plus. Opening balance is $200,000.

Teaching Consumer Concepts

SAMPLE POSTING EXAMPLES

Example: Posting a Payroll Check

Sue Smith's paycheck from Budget Plus, Inc.

Budget Plus, Inc.
430 Consumer Lane
Big Bucks, IA 00000

Check No. _____1502_____

Date _____4/2/98_____

*Pay to the
Order of* Sue B. Smith $ 875.43

eight hu

Sue Smith's savings account deposit slip.

Savings

Withdrawal   **Deposit**

Date _____4/3_____, 19 98   Cash

Name _____Sue B. Smith_____   Check Description

Address _____1282 Highland_____   From Checking

_____Big Bucks, IA 00000_____   Deposit   43 | 77

Account number _____

Amount withdrawn _____

Sign here _____

Checking Deposit Ticket

Name _____Sue B. Smith_____
       (Personal account)

Business Name _____

       (Business account)

Address _____1282 Highland_____

_____Big Bucks, IA 00000_____

Account No. _____

Date _____4/3/98_____

sign here for cash received

Big Bucks
Savings Bank

Currency

Coin

Checks (list each check separately)

Budget Plus, Inc.   875 | 43

Less Savings   43 | 77

Total   831 | 66

Less Cash Received

Net Deposit   831 | 66

Be sure each item is properly endorsed!

Sue Smith's checking account deposit slip

Step A: Post Checking Deposit

Checking Deposit Ticket

Name _____Sue B. Smith_____
       (Personal account)

Business Name _____

       (Business account)

Address _____1282 Highland_____

Big Bucks, IA 00000

Account No. _____

Date _____4/3/98_____

sign here for cash received

Big Bucks
Savings Bank

Currency

Coin

Checks (list each check separately)

Budget Plus, Inc.   875 | 43

Less Savings   43 | 77

Total   831 | 66

Less Cash Received

Net Deposit   831 | 66

95% of paycheck goes into Smith's checking account. (The other 5% will be deposited to her savings account.) Check her math.

Record the transaction on Smith's checking account statement. Because this is a deposit, the $831.66 is *credited* to her account, increasing the $400 beginning balance to $1231.66.

Big Bucks
Savings Bank
"The Friendly Bank"

Name   Sue B. Smith

Address   1282 Highland

City, State, Zip   Big Bucks, IA 00000

Statement summary for checking account # ___C-13___

Balance last statement: $ 400.00

Date	Check #	Description	Debits (−)	Credits (+)	Balance
4/3		Deposit		831.66	1,231.66

Make sure that name on deposit slip matches name on bank statement and that both forms are for checking account

Teaching Consumer Concepts

Step B: Post Savings Deposit

Savings

Withdrawal

Date _____4/3_____ , 19 _98_

Name ___Sue B. Smith___

Address ___1282 Highland___

___Big Bucks, IA 00000___

Account number ___S-13___

Amount withdrawn $ _____

Sign here _____

Big Bucks
Savings Bank

Deposit

Cash _____

Check Description _____

From Checking

Deposit _____ | 43 | 77

Total Checks _____

Less Cash Received _____

Total Deposit _____ | 43 | 77

The remaining 5% of Smith's paycheck ($43.77) goes into her savings account.

Record the transaction on Smith's savings account statement. Because this is a deposit, the $43.77 is *added* to Smith's savings, increasing the $3200 balance to $3243.77.

Make sure that name on deposit slip matches name on bank statement and that both forms are for savings account.

Name ___Sue B. Smith___

Address ___1282 Highland___

City, State, Zip ___Big Bucks, IA 00000___

Big Bucks
Savings Bank
"The Friendly Bank"

Statement summary for **savings** account # ___S-13___

Balance last statement: $ _3,200.00_

Date	Description	Withdrawal	Deposit	Interest	Balance
4/3	from Checking Deposit		43.77		3,243.77

To compute average daily balance:

Day	Date	Balance	Day	Date	Balance	Day	Date	Balance
1	3/28	3200.00	11			21		
2	3/29	3200.00	12			22		
3	3/30	3200.00	13			23		
4	3/31	3200.00	14			24		
5	4/1	3200.00	15			25		
6	4/2	3200.00	16			26		
7	4/3	3243.77	17			17		

Update the daily balance sheet to show the increase.

Step C: Post Payroll Check

The final step in posting a payroll check is to deduct it from the account on which it is drawn, or written.

Budget Plus, Inc.
430 Consumer Lane
Big Bucks, IA 00000

Check No. ___1502___

Date ___4/2/98___

Pay to the
Order of ___Sue B. Smith___ $ ___875.43___

___eight hundred seventy-five and 43/100___ **Dollars**

Big Bucks
Savings Bank

___Kyle Maxwell___
Budget Plus, Inc., Payroll Clerk

⑆071458⑆ 138472011⑆ 2428

Name on payroll check and payroll account should match.

Check number, payee, and amount should match information on check being posted.

The Budget Plus, Inc., payroll checking account balance is *debited* (reduced) by $875.43, the amount paid to Smith via check #1502. Record the transaction on the Budget Plus, Inc., payroll checking statement.

Use the date when the payroll account is debited, not the date when the check was written.

Name ___Budget Plus, Inc. – Payroll Acct.___

Address ___430 Consumer Lane___

City, State, Zip ___Big Bucks, IA 00000___

Big Bucks
Savings Bank
"The Friendly Bank"

Statement summary for **checking** account # ___B-03___

Balance last statement: $ _750,000.00_

Date	Check #	Description	Debits (–)	Credits (+)	Balance
4/3	1502	Sue B. Smith	875.43		749,124.57

Teaching Consumer Concepts

Example: Business Account Deposit

Sue Smith and Brian Koon both pay for groceries at Food Fair by writing a check. Here is what happens to those checks.

Name ___Brian Koon___   Check No. ___507___

Address ___1420 Maple Drive___
___Big Bucks, IA 00000___   Date ___4/6/98___

Pay to the
Order of ___Food Fair___ $ ___256¹⁷/₁₀₀___

___two hundred fifty-six and ¹⁷/₁₀₀___   **Dollars**

Big Bucks
Savings

Memo _____

⑈0 7 ⅃4 58⑈

Name ___Sue B. Smith___   Check No. ___501___

Address ___1282 Highland___
___Big Bucks, IA 00000___   Date ___4/6/98___

Pay to the
Order of ___Food Fair___ $ ___124³⁰/₁₀₀___

___one hundred twenty-four and ³⁰/₁₀₀___   **Dollars**

Big Bucks
Savings Bank

Memo monthly food   Sue B. Smith

⑈0 7 ⅃4 58⑈   ⅃38⅃7 20⑈   2⅃ 28

Step A: Post Business Checking Deposit

Checking Deposit Ticket

Name _____
(Personal account)

Business Name ___Food Fair___
(Business account)

Address _____
___Big Bucks, IA 00000___

Account No. ___B-07___

Date ___4/7/98___

sign here for cash received

Big Bucks
Savings Bank

Currency	
Coin	
Checks (list each check separately)	
Sue Smith	124 30
Brian Koon	256 17
Total	380 47
Less Cash Received	
Net Deposit	380 47

Be sure each item is properly endorsed!

Food Fair enters each check separately on its business checking account deposit slip.

Name ___Food Fair___

Address _____

City, State, Zip ___Big Bucks, IA 00000___

Name and account number on deposit slip and statement should match. Both forms should be for checking accounts.

The total of the two checks is recorded as a single deposit, credited to Food Fair's business checking account. (Check Food Fair's math.) The transaction is recorded on Food Fair's checking account statement.

Big Bucks
Savings Bank
"The Friendly Bank"

Statement summary for **checking account #** ___B-07___

Balance last statement: $ 500.00

Date	Check #	Description	Debits (−)	Credits (+)	Balance
4/7		Deposit		380.47	880.47

Teaching Consumer Concepts

Step B: Post Personal Checks

Each personal check must be posted to the check writer's account.

Smith's checking account is debited by $124.30, the amount she spent at Food Fair. Record the transaction on her checking statement.

Name	Sue B. Smith	Check No.	501
Address	1282 Highland		
	Big Bucks, IA 00000	Date	4/6/98
Pay to the Order of	Food Fair	$	124 30/100
one hundred twenty-four and 30/100			Dollars

Big Bucks
Savings Bank

Memo _monthly food_   Sue B. Smith

⑈071458⑈ 1384720⑈

Name and number on check and statement should match.

Use the date that you debit the account, not the date on Smith's check.

Big Bucks
Savings Bank
"The Friendly Bank"

Name	Sue B. Smith
Address	1282 Highland
City, State, Zip	Big Bucks, IA 00000

Statement summary for checking account # ___C-13___

Balance last statement: $ 400.00

Date	Check #	Description	Debits (−)	Credits (+)	Balance
4/5		Deposit		831.66	1,231.66
4/7	501	Food Fair	124.30		1,107.36

Koon's checking account is debited by $256.17, the amount he spent at Food Fair. Record the transaction on his checking statement.

Name	Brian Koon	Check No.	507
Address	1420 Maple Drive		
	Big Bucks, IA 00000	Date	4/6/98
Pay to the Order of	Food Fair	$	256 17/100
two hundred fifty-six and 17/100			Dollars

Big Bucks
Savings Bank

Brian Koon

⑈071458⑈ 138472

Name and number on check and statement should match.

Use the date that you debit the account, not the date on Koon's check.

Big Bucks
Savings Bank
"The Friendly Bank"

Name	Brian Koon
Address	1420 Maple Drive
City, State, Zip	Big Bucks, IA 00000

Statement summary for checking account # ___C-09___

Balance last statement: $ 400.00

Date	Check #	Description	Debits (−)	Credits (+)	Balance
4/7	1507	Food Fair	256.17		143.83

Follow the same steps to post business checks to the Budget Plus payroll account. Remember to also post the check as a deduction on the business's checking account summary.

Teaching Consumer Concepts

Form A—Bank Account Manager/Account Description and Signature Card form

Account Description and Signature Card

Big Bucks
Savings Bank

Account Owner's Name(s) _____

Address _____ Account Number _____

City, State, Zip _____ Phone Number _____

Owner 1 Social Security Number _____ Birth Date _____

Owner 2 Social Security Number _____ Birth Date _____

****

Present Employer _____ Length of Employment _____

Address _____ Phone _____

****

Type of Account: ____ New   ____ Existing   ____ Checking   ____ Savings   ____ Business

Date opened _____ Amount of initial deposit _____

****

Authorized Signatures

Number of signatures required
for withdrawal _____

1. _____

2. _____

****

Signature—I certify under penalties of perjury that the statements made on this form are accurate and true.

_____

Date _____

Form K—Bank Account Manager/Form 1099 Interest Income form

9595   ☐ VOID   ☐ CORRECTED

PAYER'S name, street address, city, state, ZIP code, and telephone no.		**1** Rents $	OMB No. 1545-0115	**Miscellaneous Income**
		2 Royalties $	19**98**	
		3 Other income $	Form 1099-MISC	
PAYER'S Federal identification number	RECIPIENT'S identification number	**4** Federal income tax withheld $	**5** Fishing boat proceeds $	**Copy A** **For** **Internal Revenue Service Center**
RECIPIENT'S name		**6** Medical and health care payments $	**7** Nonemployee compensation $	**File with Form 1096.**
Street address (including apt. no.)		**8** Substitute payments in lieu of dividends or interest $	**9** Payer made direct sales of $5,000 or more of consumer products to a buyer (recipient) for resale ▶ ☐	For Paperwork Reduction Act Notice and instructions for completing this form,
City, state, and ZIP code		**10** Crop insurance proceeds $	**11** State income tax withheld $	see **Instructions for Forms 1099, 1098,**
Account number (optional)	2nd TIN Not. ☐	**12** State/Payer's state number	**13 Interest Income** $	**5498, and W-2G.**

Form **1099-MISC**   48-0971237   Department of the Treasury - Internal Revenue Service

Do NOT Cut or Separate Forms on This Page

     Teaching Consumer Concepts

Form B—Bank Account Manager/Check Register form

Check Register

Personal Check Register Business Checking Ledger for _____

Check No.	Date	Description of Transaction	Payment/Debit	Deposit/Credit	Balance

Form F—Bank Account Manager/Savings Passbook form

Savings Passbook

Savings Passbook for _____

Date	Interest	Deposits	Withdrawals	Balance

Teaching Consumer Concepts

Form C—Bank Account Manager/Check: Business or Personal form

Name _____   *Check No.* _____

Address _____

_____   *Date* _____

Pay to the
Order of _____ $ _____

_____ **Dollars**

Big Bucks
Savings Bank

Memo _____   _____

⑈⑈O⑈⑈⑈4⑈58⑈⑈   ⑈38⑈4720⑈⑈   2⑈28

Form D—Bank Account Manager/Checking Deposit Ticket form

Checking Deposit Ticket

Name _____
(Personal account)

Business Name _____

_____
(Business account)

Address _____

_____

Account No. _____

Date _____

_____
sign here for cash received

Big Bucks
Savings Bank

Currency		
Coin		
Checks (list each check separately)		
Total		
Less Cash Received		
Net Deposit		

Be sure each item is properly endorsed!

Form E—Bank Account Manager/Savings Deposit Ticket form

Savings

Withdrawal   **Deposit**

Date _____ , 19 _____

Name _____

Address _____

_____

Account number _____

Amount withdrawn $ _____

Sign here _____

Big Bucks
Savings Bank

Cash		
Check Description		
Total Checks		
Less Cash Received		
Total Deposit		

Teaching Consumer Concepts

Checking Account Statement

Name _____

Address _____

City, State, Zip _____

**Big Bucks
Savings Bank**
"The Friendly Bank"

Statement summary for checking account # _____

Balance last statement: $ _____

Date	Check #	Description	Debits (−)	Credits (+)	Balance

Service charge: $5.00   **Current Balance $** _____

Teaching Consumer Concepts

Form H—Bank Account Manager/Checking Account Reconciliation form

Checking Account Reconciliation

Month _____ , 19 ____

OUTSTANDING CHECKS—NOT CHARGED TO ACCOUNT

DESCRIPTION	AMOUNT
TOTAL	**$**

Bank balance shown on this statement: _____

Add deposits not credited on
        this statement: _____

_____

_____

Total: _____

Subtract checks outstanding
        (total from list) _____

Balance: This should agree with your
        check register after deducting
        any bank charges. _____

Form J—Bank Account Manager/Savings Account Reconciliation form

Savings Account Reconciliation

Month _____ , 19 ____

Bank balance shown on this statement: _____

Add deposits not credited on this statement: _____

_____

Total: _____

Subtract withdrawals outstanding _____

Balance: This should agree with your savings book after adding
        any interest earned. _____

In Case of Errors or Questions

Call, write, or come see us in person as soon as you can if you think your statement is in error. We must hear from you no later than four days after we sent you the statement. Describe the error or the transfer you are unsure about and explain why you believe it is an error or why you need more information. Tell us the dollar amount of the suspected error. We reserve the right to require a written description of the complaint. We will tell you the results of our investigation in writing within five business days.

Teaching Consumer Concepts

Form I—Bank Account Manager/Savings Account Statement form

Savings Account Statement

Name _____

Address _____

City, State, Zip _____

Big Bucks
Savings Bank
"The Friendly Bank"

Statement summary for savings account # _____

Balance last statement: $ _____

Date	Description	Withdrawal	Deposit	Interest	Balance

To compute average daily balance:

Day	Date	Balance	Day	Date	Balance	Day	Date	Balance
1	____	_____	11	____	_____	21	____	_____
2	____	_____	12	____	_____	22	____	_____
3	____	_____	13	____	_____	23	____	_____
4	____	_____	14	____	_____	24	____	_____
5	____	_____	15	____	_____	25	____	_____
6	____	_____	16	____	_____	26	____	_____
7	____	_____	17	____	_____	27	____	_____
8	____	_____	18	____	_____	28	____	_____
9	____	_____	19	____	_____	29	____	_____
10	____	_____	20	____	_____	30	____	_____
						31	____	_____

_____ ÷ _____ = _____
Sum of Daily Balance   Number of days   Average Daily Balance

Interest Computation:

p Average daily balance: _____

r Interest rate: _____3.5%_____

t Compounded monthly: _____$\frac{1}{12}$_____

I Interest Earned; p*r*t _____   Current Balance $ _____

Teaching Consumer Concepts

Car Dealer

Job Description: Helps customers purchase new and used vehicles. Fills out all car sale paperwork, including purchase agreements and disclosure statements. Collects down payment at the time of the sale and final payment when buyers have arranged financing.

Educational Requirements: Minimum of two years of post-secondary education and six months of previous sales experience.

Benefits: Earnings are based on salary plus commissions. Base salary—$10,000, plus 1 percent commission on the first $50,000 in sales and 2 percent commission on sales over $50,000 each month. Health insurance coverage provided—individual. Shopping allowance—$1,000 (new employees only). Sick days—two per quarter. Personal days—five per year. Additional benefits—company car (Car Dealer pays maintenance and insurance).

Duties

Choose a Car

Help customers find a car that suits their family size, income level, and tastes, and explain guarantees (*New cars:* six years or 60,000 miles, whichever comes first. *Used cars:* no guarantee, sold "as is.")

Agree on a Purchase Price

Vehicles sell for the price listed in the dealer's description, unless the dealer and the buyer negotiate a lower price. (Remember, any decrease you agree to in the price of a car also affects the commission that you might earn that month.)

Complete a Purchase Agreement (Form A; see sample, page 51).

1. General Information: Complete all information required about the buyer(s) and the car.
2. Down Payment:
   - A down payment of at least 20 percent of the agreed purchase price is due with the application.

- A trade-in is considered part of the down payment. (All students have a car to trade in. The trade-in value of all cars is $1,500.)
- Compute the difference between the 20 percent down payment needed and the $1,500 trade-in value to determine how much cash the buyer must put down.

3. Cash Balance Due on Delivery (This is the final amount that you collect from buyers after they have arranged financing and are ready to drive off in the newly-purchased vehicle. It may be more or less than the amount that the bank will actually lend on a particular vehicle. Here is how to compute cash balance due on delivery):
   - List the *purchase price*.
   - Subtract the *trade-in value* of $1,500.
   - Add 6 percent *sales tax*.
   - Add *title fee* ($15 charge for transferring title to new owners).
   - Subtract the *additional cash down* (see Down Payment, above).

4. Signatures: Explain the trade-in certification and warranties sections and have one of the buyers sign each section. Car dealer and *all* buyers must sign the bottom of the purchase agreement.

5. Additional Cash Down: Get buyer's check for additional cash down when the purchase agreement is signed.

Fill Out Disclosure Statements (Form B) for the Car Purchased

- Damage Disclosure: Assume no cars have been damaged in an accident.
- Odometer (total mileage) Disclosure: Assume no odometers have been tampered with.
- Paste a copy of the car advertisement to the bottom of this form. Cut from the second copy of the car listings.

Other Duties

- Send customers to the Loan Officer. If a loan is required, customers can borrow up to 80 percent of the purchase price from the bank, or they can borrow money from the cash value of a life insurance policy. Some customers will pay the cash balance due on delivery from their savings to avoid the interest on a loan. They need to transfer the money from savings to checking so they can pay you.
- Collect the cash balance due on delivery as soon as the money is transferred or the loan is approved.
- Send customers to the County Treasurer to get their registration.

Teaching Consumer Concepts

Complete the Accounts Receivable Card

Create a separate accounts receivable card for each sale.
1. Enter Amount Due: For each sale enter the total of the *additional cash down*, and the *cash balance due on delivery*.
2. Enter Account Paid: As you collect each check, enter the amount of the payment and the check number on the appropriate accounts receivable card and compute the new balance. (The *additional cash down* would be entered immediately as a payment when you create an accounts receivable card, because you would already have the buyer's first check in hand.)

Enter All Transactions in the Business Checking Ledger

1. Enter deposits daily:
   - Fill out a business checking deposit slip for all checks received that day.
   - Record the total deposit in the checking ledger.
   - Be sure that all checks are endorsed "For deposit only to the account of Colden's Cool Cars."
   - Staple deposit slip and checks together and give to Bank Account Manager or leave in deposit drop box.
2. Reimburse Budget Plus, Inc.—Payroll Account:
   - Make out check for 80 percent of the daily deposit.
   - Record the check in the checking ledger.
   - Give the check to the Budget Plus Payroll Clerk.

Complete the Commission Statement

- After you complete a purchase agreement, record the purchase price on the Commission Statement. When all students in the simulation have purchased a vehicle, total the sales to compute your commission.
  Commission = Amount of Purchase × Commission Rate, or 1 percent of the first $50,000 in sales each month, and 2 percent on all sales over $50,000 in one month.
- Give the Commission Statement to the Payroll Clerk to be included in your next paycheck.

SAMPLE MOTOR VEHICLE PURCHASE AGREEMENT

Motor Vehicle Purchase Agreement

Date _3/7/98_ Salesperson _Mike Lutz_

Buyer _Carl Porter_ Buyer's Birth Month _June_

Co-buyer _Mae Porter_ Phone Number _(319) 555-0001_

Address _1477 E. Platt, Big Bucks, IA 00000_

Description of Vehicle Purchased
_X_ New _____ Used

Year _1998_ Make _Chevy_ Model _Lumina Sedan_

Body Type: _X_ Car _____ Pickup _____ Van _____ Other VIN _____ 8K3902IUJ29 _____
(Vehicle Identification Number)

Down Payment Computation

Purchase Price	$17,500.00
Minimum Down Payment: Purchase Price × 20%	3,500.00
Trade-in Allowance	**$1,500.00**

Additional Cash Down Payment Required
If trade-in allowance is less than minimum down payment, enter the difference; otherwise enter "0." ____ 2,000.00

Price agreed on after negotiation

Collect this amount now

Cash Balance Computations

Purchase Price	17,500.00
Subtract: Trade-in Allowance	**$1,500.00**
Taxable Amount	16,000.00
Add: Sales Tax (6%)	960.00
Title Fee:	15.00
Total Cash Price	16,975.00
Subtract: Additional Cash Down Payment	2,000.00
Cash Balance Due on Delivery	$14,975.00

Collect this after the car loan is approved

Buyer's Trade-in Certification:
1. The vehicle was never salvaged or rebuilt.
2. The odometer reading is accurate and correct to the best of my knowledge.
3. The following are all in good working condition and meet the manufacturer's specifications: emission control system, engine, transmission, head, block, power train, and frame.
4. Any claims I have made as to the condition of this vehicle are true and correct.

x _Carl Porter_

Warranties: I understand that the vehicle I am buying is being sold under the following conditions:
_X_ With a warranty, provided by the manufacturer. The car dealership is not a party to this warranty.
_____ As is, with no warranty either implied or expressed.

x _Carl Porter_

This contract is for educational purposes only. It represents the complete agreement regardless of any previous agreements, either oral or written. I certify that I am at least 18 years of age, that I have read this contract and voluntarily agree to its terms.

Carl Porter Buyer's Signature _000-11-2222_ SS#

Mae Porter Co-buyer's Signature _712-12-1212_ SS#

Accepted by: _Mike Lutz_ **Date** _3/7/98_
an authorized Colden's Cool Cars Representative

Teaching Consumer Concepts

COLDEN'S COOL CARS

Push, Pull, or Drag Sale
$1,500 minimum trade-in allowance on any vehicle in stock

1999 Jeep Wrangler 4 × 4, convertible, tilt, white letter tires, 5-spoke steel wheels; Odometer reading: 500; VIN: 749J893GFA8; Weight: 3,200; Symbol: 10; Gas mileage: 20; List: $24,700, now offered at $21,995

1999 Lincoln/Mercury Sable GS, remote entry system, ABS, A/C, tilt, cruise, cassette, power windows and locks; Odometer reading: 500; VIN: 2379J8FL99; Weight: 3,300; Symbol: 6; Gas mileage: 25; List: $19,000, now offered at $18,999

1999 Buick LeSabre Custom, 3800 Series II, V6, dual air bags, ABS, A/C, stereo/cassette; Odometer reading: 500; VIN: 23KJ9GJ49E99; Weight: 3,500; Symbol: 8; Gas mileage: 24; List: $22,900, now offered at $22,796

1998 Ford Ranger XLT, A/C, AM/FM, cassette; Odometer reading: 16,780; VIN: 289KFE96OB88; Weight: N/A; Symbol: 11; Gas mileage: 19; List: $11,200, now offered at $10,575

1998 Chevy Lumina sedan, V6, dual air bags, aluminum wheels, A/C, PW & PL; Odometer reading: 18,703; VIN: 81K39021UJ29; Weight: 3,400; Symbol: 6; Gas mileage: 24; List: $19,000, now offered at $16,897

1997 Buick Century, V6, auto, PW & PL, air bag, AM/FM, cassette, A/C, tilt; Odometer reading: 28,000; VIN: 28RY783674G6; Weight: 3,000; Symbol: 6; Gas mileage: 24; List: $18,000, now offered at $11,499

1997 Chevy GeoPrism, auto, PW & PL, AM/FM cassette, dual air bags, A/C, rear defogger; Odometer reading: 42,370; VIN: 49JF83934K523; Weight: 2,300; Symbol: 11; Gas mileage: 32; List: $13,000, now offered at $10,995

1996 Ford Taurus, 4-door, sporty, loaded, moon roof; Odometer reading: 68,453; VIN: 39TJ949U892148; Weight: 3,300; Symbol: 4; Gas mileage: 25; List: $19,800, now offered at $12,995

1996 Chevy Cavalier, one owner, 4 cyl, A/C, tilt, sporty; Odometer reading; 57,784; VIN: 435J74F43C97; Weight: 2,500; Symbol: 5; Gas mileage: 27; List: $9,600, now offered at $8,399

1995 Dodge Intrepid, V6, PW & PL, A/C, AM/FM, cassette, one owner, emerald green; Odometer reading: 48,853; VIN: 785RCV999H3; Weight: 4,400; Symbol: 8; Gas mileage: 24; List: $20,700, now offered at $11,999

1995 Chevy Corsica, V6, PW & PL, tilt, cruise, A/C, cassette; Odometer reading: 64,847; VIN: 85D53W3J800; Weight: 2,600; Symbol: 7; Gas mileage: 26; List: $12,000, now offered at $7,999

1994 Chevy Cavalier, 2-dr, A/C, sunroof, AM/FM, cassette, aqua teal; Odometer reading: 42,342; VIN: 4572H645E42; Weight: 2,700; Symbol: 8; Gas mileage: 28; List: $13,000, now offered at $6,999

1993 Ford Tempo, automatic, A/C, 4-door, silver; Odometer reading: 63,555; VIN: 453H427D454; Weight: 2,500; Symbol: 4; Gas mileage: 23; List: $8,500, now offered at $5,995

1992 Ford Probe, 4-cyl, auto, AM/FM, economy at its best! Odometer reading: 72,854; Weight: 2,400; Symbol: 4; Gas mileage: 27; List: $9,900, now offered at $4,899

Teaching Consumer Concepts

Motor Vehicle Purchase Agreement

Date _____ Salesperson _____

Buyer _____ Buyer's Birth Month _____

Co-buyer _____ Phone Number _____

Address _____

Description of Vehicle Purchased ____ New ____ Used

Year _____ Make _____ Model _____

Body Type: ____ Car ____ Pickup ____ Van ____ Other VIN _____
(Vehicle Identification Number)

Down Payment Computation

Purchase Price .... _____

Minimum Down Payment: Purchase Price × 20% .... _____

Trade-in Allowance $1,500.00

Additional Cash Down Payment Required
   If trade-in allowance is less than minimum down payment,
   enter the difference; otherwise enter "0." .... _____

Cash Balance Computations

Purchase Price .... _____

   Subtract: Trade-in Allowance $1,500.00

Taxable Amount .... _____

   Add: Sales Tax (6%) .... _____

   Title Fee: .... _____

Total Cash Price .... _____

   Subtract: Additional Cash Down Payment .... _____

Cash Balance Due on Delivery .... _____

Buyer's Trade-in Certification:

1. The vehicle was never salvaged or rebuilt.
2. The odometer reading is accurate and correct to the best of my knowledge.
3. The following are all in good working condition and meet the manufacturer's specifications: emission control system, engine, transmission, head, block, power train, and frame.
4. Any claims I have made as to the condition of this vehicle are true and correct.

X _____

Warranties: I understand that the vehicle I am buying is being sold under the following conditions:
_____ With a warranty, provided by the manufacturer. The car dealership is not a party to this warranty.
_____ As is, with no warranty either implied or expressed.

X _____

This contract is for educational purposes only. It represents the complete agreement regardless of any previous agreements, either oral or written. I certify that I am at least 18 years of age, that I have read this contract and voluntarily agree to its terms.

_____ Buyer's Signature _____SS#

Co-buyer's Signature _____SS#

Accepted by: _____ **Date** _____
an authorized Colden's Cool Cars Representative

Teaching Consumer Concepts

Form B—Car Dealer/Damage Disclosure Statement form

Damage Disclosure Statement

I _____ (Colden's Cool Cars Dealer) certify the following damage disclosure statement is true and correct.

Year: _____ Make: _____ Model: _____

VIN: _____

   1. This motor vehicle has sustained damage of $3,000 or more.
      _____ yes _____ no   If yes, amount of damage: _____

   2. I am aware that this motor vehicle was salvaged or rebuilt.
      _____ yes _____ no   If yes, _____ salvaged _____ rebuilt _____ previous state where titled

x _____   _____
      Authorized Colden's Cool Cars Dealer   Date

x _____   _____
      Buyer's Signature   Date

Form C—Car Dealer/Odometer Disclosure Statement form

Odometer Disclosure Statement

Year: _____ Make: _____ Model: _____

VIN: _____

The odometer currently reads _____.

_____ This reflects the actual mileage of the vehicle, to the best of my knowledge.

_____ Warning: The odometer reading has been tampered with or for some other reason does not reflect the actual mileage of the vehicle.

x _____   _____
      Authorized Colden's Cool Cars Dealer   Date

x _____   _____
      Buyer's Signature   Date

Paste Car Advertisement Here

Teaching Consumer Concepts

Child Care Worker

Job Description: Provides care for young children in a center setting; helps them eat, dress, and learn social skills. Plans recreational and educational activities. Maintains registration forms for each child and computes monthly day care bills.

Education Requirements: High school diploma.

Benefits: Beginning salary—$15,000. Free day care for employee's children. Health insurance coverage provided—individual. Shopping allowance—$1,000 (new employees only). Sick days—two per quarter. Personal days—five per year.

Duties

Handle Registration

Have parents complete a registration (Form A) for each child they have in day care, and check that the forms are filled out completely. These forms contain emergency phone numbers; keep them handy.

Daily Planning

Complete at least five days' worth of instructional and activity plans (Form B) that involve children in such group activities as singing, reading, playing games, coloring, presenting puppet shows, and making crafts. The activities, which are interspersed with free time, should enhance social skills, improve large or fine motor skills and coordination, promote personal hygiene, teach basic concepts such as number and letter recognition, or improve self-esteem. (Give these plans to your teacher when completed.)

Prepare Monthly Day Care Bills (Form C)

1. Fill in the parent's name, address, and phone number on the invoice.
2. List each child's name and age. (If parents have one child, it is an infant; two children, an infant and a three-year-old; three children, an infant, a two- or three-year-old, and a five- or six-year old.)

3. Check Registration Form to see whether the family is in Plan A (income over $20,000) or Plan B (income under $20,000). List the daily rate for each child (see rate sheet, p. 57). If parents have two children, use the "1st Child" rate for the oldest and the "Each Additional Child" rate for the youngest. If there is a third child, add the "Before- and After-School" rate.

4. Convert the daily rate to a monthly rate. Assume that the child attends 5 days per week, 52 weeks per year. (For convenience, assume that school-age children attend school year round, so the rate for their care stays the same.) Multiply the daily rate by 5 and by 52, then divide the answer by 12 to determine the monthly amount. Add in the laundry fee, if applicable, and total the charges.

Complete Accounts Receivable Cards

Create a separate accounts receivable card for each family.

1. Enter Amount Due: For each family, enter the total monthly amount due.
2. Enter Amount Paid: As you collect each check, enter the amount of the payment and the check number on that family's accounts receivable card and compute the new balance.

Enter All Transactions in the Business Checking Ledger

1. Enter deposits daily:
   - Fill out a business checking deposit slip for all checks received that day.
   - Record the total deposit in the checking ledger.
   - Be sure that all checks are endorsed "For deposit only to the account of Bubba Bear Day Care."
   - Staple deposit slip and checks together and give to Bank Account Manager or leave in deposit drop box.
2. Reimburse Budget Plus, Inc.—Payroll Account:
   - Make out a check for 80 percent of the daily deposit.
   - Record the check in the checking ledger.
   - Give the check to the Budget Plus Payroll Clerk.

Bubba Bear Day Care
Rates
effective August 1, 1998

Plan A rates apply to families with incomes above $20,000. Plan B rates apply to families with incomes below $20,000, and are for full-time and after-school care only.

	1st Child		Each Additional Child	
	Plan A	Plan B	Plan A	Plan B
Ages 3 through 11 (must be 3 by September 1)				
Full day (5 to 12 hours)	$15.30	$12.75	$11.90	$10.65
Half day (5 hours or less)	9.90	8.25	7.70	6.90
Minimum weekly charge (2 half days)	19.80	16.50	15.40	13.80
Ages Infant through 2				
Full day (5 to 12 hours)	$16.15	$14.90	$12.35	$11.05
Half day (5 hours or less)	10.45	9.65	8.00	7.15
Minimum weekly charge (2 half days)	20.90	19.30	16.00	14.30
Before- and after-school program:	$6.30	$5.25	$6.30	$5.25

Laundry fee*—Plan A only per child:

  Infant through 2 years old $3.50 monthly

  3 through 4 years old   2.50 monthly

Extra Charges:

  Approximately $4 per child for Holiday project.

  $15 per check returned.

  $5 per 15 minutes (or fraction of), per child picked up after closing (6:00 P.M.).

*No laundry fee is assessed for Plan B children or for those in before- and after-school care only.

Teaching Consumer Concepts

Form A—Child Care Worker/Registration form

BUBBA BEAR DAY CARE
Registration Form (please print)

Child's Full Name _____

Address _____

City_____ State _____ Zip _____

Home Phone _____

Date of Birth _____ Age _____ Sex _____

Nickname_____Hand Preference _____

Name	Brothers	Age	Name	Sisters	Age
_____		_____	_____		_____
_____		_____	_____		_____
_____		_____	_____		_____

Father's Name _____

Employer_____ City _____

Work Phone_____ Occupation _____

Mother's Name _____

Employer_____ City _____

Work Phone_____ Occupation _____

Family Physician _____ Phone_____

Address_____

Allergies _____

<u>Parental Permission for Emergency Medical/Surgical Care.</u>

Parent's Signature _____

<u>Permission to administer Tylenol or Motrin, if necessary.</u>

Brand Preference _____ Parent's Signature_____

<u>Field Trip Permission</u>

Parent's Signature _____

Who has authority to pick up your child?

1. _____ Phone # _____

2. _____ Phone # _____

3. _____ Phone # _____

EMERGENCY PHONE NUMBER (if parents cannot be reached)

Name _____ Phone # _____

Name _____ Phone # _____

GROSS FAMILY INCOME if reduced rates are requested _____

Form B—Child Care Worker/Daily Planner form

Daily Planner

Employee: _____ Date: _____

Age Level: _____

Goals:

Areas of Development:

____ Educational ____ Physical ____ Social ____ Emotional

Planned Activities:

Instructional Materials Required:

Comments:

Form C—Child Care Worker/Invoice form

BUBBA BEAR DAY CARE
Invoice

Account Name _____ Phone Number _____

Address _____

Child	Age	Daily Rate	Monthly Rate

LAUNDRY FEES (Plan A only) _____

TOTAL DUE _____

If you have questions regarding this billing, contact our office. There is a $15 fee for returned checks. Households making less than $20,000 may be eligible for reduced rates. Contact the office for more information.

Teaching Consumer Concepts

County Treasurer

Job Description: Determines car registration fees on the basis of a car's list price and weight. Determines real estate tax amounts for home owners on the basis of a home's assessed value.

Educational Requirements: Undergraduate degree in political science or public administration.

Benefits: Starting salary—$28,000, with semiannual reviews. Shopping allowance—$1,000 (new employees only). Health insurance coverage provided—individual. Sick days—two per quarter. Personal days—five per year.

Duties

Determine Car Registration Fee

1. Determine the age, weight, and list price of the car by looking at the Car Dealer's vehicle list. Use the chart below to determine what percentages to use in the annual fee formula. (For pickups, the annual registration fee is a flat $65.00.)

Age of Car*	Percent of Weight	Percent of List Price
1–5 YEARS	40	100
6 YEARS	40	75
7–8 YEARS	40	50
9 YEARS	40	10

*1999 is considered 1 year old for registration fees.

2. Compute the annual registration fee:

$$\text{FEE} = \frac{(\text{Weight} \times \text{Percent of Weight}) + (\text{List Price} \times \text{Percent of List Price})}{100}$$

3. Complete the Registration Fee billing form (Form A). Remind customers to list this bill as an annual expense under their birth month.

Determine Real Estate Taxes (Form B)

Real estate taxes are used to support local schools, maintain local and county parks and roads, and pay the costs of local and county government.

1. Determine the assessed value of the house.

- Find its market value (the house's listed price in the Realtor's house listings).
- Determine the rate of assessment. If the market value is less than $50,000, the rate of assessment is 95 percent. If the market value is $50,000 or more, the rate is 85 percent.
- Compute the assessed value:
  Assessed Value = Rate of Assessment × Market Value.

2. Calculate real estate taxes, using 19.5 *mills*/dollar as the tax rate for Big Bucks (a mill = $0.001):
   Annual Real Estate Tax = Tax Rate × Assessed Value
   (Round your answer to the nearest dollar.)
   - Real estate taxes are payable semiannually, in March and September. Divide the taxes by 2 to determine how much is due with each payment.
   - Make out the bill. All customers get the Homestead Exemption because their home is their primary place of residence.

NOTE: Customers do not need to write out a check for these taxes, but must list the amount on their cash flow summary as an expense in March and September.

Complete the Accounts Receivable Cards

Use one card per employee for car registrations and another card per home owner(s) for real estate taxes.

1. Enter Amount Due. For each employee, enter the amount of the annual car registration fee. For home owners, enter the amount of the semiannual real estate tax bills.
2. Enter Account Paid. As you collect each check for car registrations, enter the amount of the payment and the check number on the appropriate accounts receivable card and compute the new balance. Because you will not receive checks for real estate taxes, those cards will show an outstanding balance due.

Enter All Transactions in the Business Checking Ledger

1. Enter deposits daily:
   - Fill out a business checking deposit slip for all checks received that day.
   - Record the total deposit in the checking ledger.
   - Be sure that all checks have been endorsed "For deposit only to the account of Ward County Treasurer."
   - Staple deposit slip and checks together and give to Bank Account Manager or leave in deposit drop box.
2. Reimburse Budget Plus, Inc.—Payroll Account:
   - Make out check for 80 percent of the daily deposit.
   - Record the check in the checking ledger.
   - Give the check to the Payroll Clerk.

Teaching Consumer Concepts

Form A—County Treasurer/Registration Fee form

Ward County Treasurer's Office
_____, Treasurer
Big Bucks, Iowa

Owner:

Name _____ SS# _____ Birth Month _____

Address _____ Phone # _____

City, State, Zip _____

Car Registration:

Year _____ Make _____ Model _____

Body Type   Car _____   Pickup _____   Van _____   VIN _____

List Price _____ Weight _____ Age in Years _____

Percent of List Price _____ Percent of Weight _____

Pay this amount   ➞   **Annual Registration Fee: $** _____

Due in your birth month.   _Make checks payable to Ward County Treasurer_

Form B—County Treasurer/Real Estate Tax form

Ward County Treasurer's Office
_____, Treasurer
Big Bucks, Iowa

HOME OWNER

Name: _____ Homestead Exemption: Y or N

Address: _____ Phone #: _____

City, State, Zip: _____ SS#: _____

RESIDENCE

Address: _____

Market Value: _____

TAX COMPUTATION

Rate of Assessment: _____%   Assessed Value: $ _____

Tax Rate:_____mills/$ Annual Taxes Due: $ _____

Semiannual Payments Due in March & September $ _____

Teaching Consumer Concepts

Department Store Manager

Job Description: Uses department store catalogs or sale advertisements to help customers select clothing, furniture, appliances, and other items for purchase. (All employees must spend their $1,000 shopping allowance at the department store.) Computes order forms for all purchases. Computes the total of each customer's purchases, including sales tax and, when applicable, interest for credit card charges. Either collects cash for payment or charges purchases to the department store credit card for monthly payoff. Should have good working knowledge of three or more catalogs, and have several sale flyers and classified ads available for bargain hunters.

Education Requirements: Undergraduate degree in marketing or business administration. Previous sales management experience is helpful.

Benefits: Earnings are based on salary plus commissions. Base salary—$15,000 per year plus commission of 5 percent on required purchases and 10 percent on luxury purchases. Health insurance coverage provided—individual. Shopping allowance—$1,000 (new employees only). Sick days—two per quarter. Personal days—five per year.

Duties

Help Customers Make Purchases

1. Required purchases ("needs"). Make sure that customers make all required purchases, as follows:
   - Clothing—Each family member must have enough clothing to last seven days. Items purchased must include underwear, socks, shoes, dress clothes, casual clothes, sleepers, a winter coat, boots, hats, gloves, and a lightweight jacket.
   - Living room—Customers must purchase at least one couch, two chairs, and a television.
   - Bedroom—All family members must have a bed; infants must have a crib. Dressers or under-bed storage drawers are recommended but not required.
   - Dining room—A table and four chairs are required.
   - Appliances and kitchen utensils—Households must have dishes, glasses, silverware, pots, and pans. In addition, apartment

dwellers must have a microwave oven and homeowners must have a microwave, refrigerator, stove, and washing machine.
- Miscellaneous—Families with children must have car seats and age-appropriate toys.

2. Luxury purchases. Anything not on the "required" list is considered a luxury item. Such items include stereos, clothes dryers, VCRs, floor lamps, computers, exercise equipment, etc. The commission rate for these items is double that for required purchases.

3. Alternative purchases/bargain hunting. Customers may find nonstore advertisements (classified or "shoppers" newspaper ads) for items they wish to purchase that are selling at lower prices elsewhere. They can bring these ads to the Department Store Manager and purchase the items at the lower price; a copy of the ad must be attached to the purchase order form. However, these items are not under warranty, which could be a problem if they break down.

Compute Customer's Bills (Form A)

- List all required purchases (separate department store purchases from alternative purchases).
- List all luxury purchases (separate department store purchases from alternative purchases).
- Total regular department store purchases. Add 6 percent sales tax to get a subtotal.
- Total alternative purchases. Do not add sales tax to alternative purchases.
- Add subtotal (department store purchases plus sales tax) and alternative purchases, subtract $1,000 from the total, and calculate the balance due.
- Customers can pay the balance due in one of three ways:
  1. They can pay the entire balance in a lump sum payment.
  2. They can spread the balance into 12 equal payments over a year. (Customers make out a check for the first monthly payment only. They note the balance in their cash flow summary.)
  3. They can make installment payments on a department store credit card and pay the balance plus interest over a three-year period. Collect a check for the first monthly payment. Inform customers they should use this amount as the monthly payment on their cash flow summary.

Credit Card Purchases

Customers who choose the third payment option must apply for a department store credit card.
- Have the customer complete a credit card application (Form B).
- Use the following criteria to determine the monthly payment:

1. A three-year (36-month) term for repayments.
2. 18% annual percentage rate (1.5 percent per month.) Determine the monthly payment by using the monthly payment table, a formula, a business calculator, or a computer program. (You should have a copy of the table and calculation instructions. Ask your teacher which method you should use.)
3. Fill out the credit card billing statement (Form C) and collect the first month's payment.

Complete the Accounts Receivable Cards

Create a separate accounts receivable card for each customer.

1. Enter Amount Due: For each customer, enter the payment due this billing cycle.
2. Enter Amount Paid: As you collect each check, enter the payment amount and the check number on the appropriate accounts receivable card and compute the new balance.
3. If monthly payments are made, list the total balance due and the number of years that payments will be made on the bottom of the card.

Enter All Transactions in the Business Checking Ledger

1. Enter deposits daily.
   - Fill out a business checking deposit slip, for all checks received that day.
   - Record the total deposit in the checking ledger.
   - Be sure that all checks are endorsed "For deposit only to the account of Heart & Home Department Store."
   - Staple deposit slip and checks together and give to Bank Account Manager or leave in deposit drop box.
2. Reimburse Budget Plus, Inc.—Payroll Account:
   - Make out a check for 80 percent of the daily deposit.
   - Record the check in the checking ledger.
   - Give the check to the Budget Plus Payroll Clerk.

Complete the Commission Statement

1. After you complete a purchase invoice, record the purchase on the Commission Statement. When all students have made their purchases, total up the sales and compute your commission. (Remember to separate required purchases from luxury purchases.) Commission = Amount of Purchase × Commission Rate, or 5 percent of the total required purchases and 10 percent of the total luxury purchases.
2. Give the Commission Statement to the Payroll Clerk to be included in your next paycheck.

Teaching Consumer Concepts

Form A—Department Store Manager/Sales Invoice form

♥ Heart & Home Department Store ♥

Sold To:

Name: _____

Address: _____

Date: _____

Invoice Number: _____

Salesperson: _____

QUANT.	DESCRIPTION OF ITEM	CATALOG	PAGE #	UNIT PRICE	TOTAL PRICE	CHECK IF APPLICABLE		
						NEED	LUXURY	ALTERNATIVE PURCHASE

Total—Department store purchases $ _____

Sales tax   _____

Subtotal   _____

Total—Alternative purchases $ _____

Grand total: _____

Less $1,000 allowance   _____

Balance due $ _____

Total Price of "Needs": _____ × 5% = _____ Commission

Total Price of "Luxuries": _____ × 10% = _____ Commission

TOTAL SALES _____   TOTAL COMMISSION _____

Form B—Department Store Manager/Credit Card Application form

♥ *Heart & Home Department Store* ♥
Credit Card Application

♥♥♥

Name: _____ Date: _____

Address: _____ Phone: _____

City, State, Zip: _____

Social Security #: _____ Birth Date: _____

♥♥♥

Check which of the following accounts you have: _____ Checking   _____ Savings

Name and Address of Financial Institution: _____

♥♥♥

List all outstanding loans and current liabilities:

Name	Type	Amount
example: Wheatland Bank	Student Loan	$8,000

List the names, addresses, and phone numbers of three references:

1. _____
2. _____
3. _____

♥♥♥

The statements made above are accurate and true to the best of my knowledge.

Applicant's Signature: _____ Co-Applicant's Signature: _____

Form C—Department Store Manager/Credit Card Statement form

♥ *Heart & Home Department Store* ♥
Statement of Credit Card Purchases

Buyer's Name: _____ Date: _____

Address: _____

Salesperson: _____ Invoice Number: _____

♥♥♥

Total Purchases	$ _____
Less shopping allowance	$ _____
Amount paid today	$ _____
Unpaid balance billed to credit card	$ _____
Interest rate:	1.5% per month*
Minimum monthly payment (due the 15th of every month)	$ _____

*18% annual percentage rate   *Thank you for your business!!*

Grocery Store Manager

Job Description: Determines monthly food bill for customers on the basis of their age, eating habits, and size of household. Handles inventory control, schedules employee hours, computes markup on goods sold.

Education Requirements: Undergraduate degree in business administration, with a major in marketing.

Benefits: Beginning salary—$24,000, with semiannual reviews. Shopping allowance—$1,000 (new employees only). Health insurance coverage—individual. Sick days—two per quarter. Personal days—five per year.

Duties

Determine Monthly Food Bills (Form A)

1. Enter the current month and customer information and have the customer choose a food plan from those listed below that suits his or her eating habits.

FOOD PLAN
Liberal: A "meat and potatoes" plan that includes some steaks and some convenience foods.
Moderate: Includes less expensive cuts of meat and fewer convenience foods.
Low cost: Has few or no convenience foods; more rice, grains, pasta, and potatoes; fewer and cheaper cuts of meat.
Thrifty: (AVAILABLE ONLY WITH TEACHER APPROVAL.) For families earning less than $16,000, similar to a food stamp program.

2. List each family member's name, sex, and age on Form A. (If two unrelated people share an apartment, each must have a separate food bill.) Include pets on the list.
3. List the monthly cost for each individual in the household from the following monthly food costs chart.

Monthly Food Costs per Household Member

	Thrifty Plan	Low-Cost Plan	Moderate Plan	Liberal Plan
Children				
1–2 years	$60.10	$74.00	$86.70	$105.10
3–5 years	64.80	80.20	99.20	118.70
6–8 years	79.30	106.60	133.00	155.10
9–11 years	94.50	121.20	155.80	179.50
Male				
12–14 years	98.40	137.10	170.50	200.80
15–19 years	101.20	141.20	176.30	204.10
20–50 years	109.70	141.20	177.30	215.30
51 years and over	98.90	135.20	167.20	200.80
Female				
12–19 years	98.40	118.80	144.60	174.70
20–50 years	99.90	125.10	152.70	196.80
51 years and over	98.50	121.50	151.20	180.60
Infants				
Formula $60				
Disposable diapers $22.50				
Pets				
$30				

Prices are based on at-home meal preparation only.
The added cost of eating out is not considered.

4. Determine the percent increase or percent decrease in monthly costs for each family member based on the size of the household. Infants and pets are not counted as part of family size when calculating these percentages, because their expenses are simply a flat monthly amount.

Adjustments in Monthly Costs Based on Family Size

Family Size:

1 person: Increase the basic cost by 20 percent.

2 people: Increase the basic cost by 10 percent.

3 people: Increase the basic cost by 5 percent.

4 people: Make no change to the basic cost.

5 people: Decrease the basic cost by 5 percent.

6 people: Decrease the basic cost by 5 percent.

7 people: Decrease the basic cost by 10 percent.

5. Calculate the adjusted costs for each person. Find the total. For example, if a family at the Liberal Plan level consisted of a 22-year-old male, a 21-year-old female, and a dog, the costs would be $204.10 + $224.51 + $30, for a total of $458.61.

Complete the Accounts Receivable Cards

Create a separate accounts receivable card for each customer.
1. Enter Amount Due: For each customer, enter the amount of the monthly food bill.
2. Enter Amount Paid: As you collect each check, enter the amount of the payment and the check number on the appropriate accounts receivable card and compute the new balance.

Enter All Transactions in the Business Checking Ledger

1. Enter deposits daily
   - Fill out a business checking deposit slip for all checks received that day.
   - Record the deposit in the checking ledger.
   - Be sure that all checks are endorsed "For deposit only to the account of Food Fair."
   - Staple deposit slip and checks together and give to Bank Account Manager or leave in deposit drop box.
2. Reimburse Budget Plus, Inc.—Payroll Account:
   - Make out a check for 80 percent of the daily deposit.
   - Record the check in the ledger.
   - Give the check to the Budget Plus Payroll Clerk.

Prepare Weekly Menu and Shop for Items (Optional)

If time permits, prepare a menu for a typical week, including all drinks, snacks, and meals that you would eat. Shop for the items on your menu at two or more stores and compare prices. If possible, price some items at a discount store. Compare the price difference between name-brand items and generic or store-brand items. Look for coupons to increase your savings. Make a presentation to class about your menu and the findings from your comparison shopping.

Teaching Consumer Concepts

Food Fair, Inc.

Billing for the Month of _____

Name _____ Phone _____

Address _____

City, State, Zip: _____

Food Plan _____ Number in Household _____

Name	M/F	Age	Base Cost	+/− Percent	Adjusted Cost

Total Monthly Food Bill: $ _____

Teaching Consumer Concepts

Housing Coordinator

Job Description: Helps customers find suitable housing to purchase (Realtor) or rent (Leasing Agent). Fills out appropriate purchase agreements or leases. Helps arrange financing for purchases. Collects housing payments. Handles two business checking accounts—one for the real estate business and one for the leasing business.

Education Requirements: High school diploma plus a minimum of three years post-secondary education in business administration, finance, or marketing; a real estate agent's license valid for the state in which the agent does business.

Benefits: Earnings are based on salary plus commissions. Base salary— $10,000 per year, plus 6 percent commission on gross real estate sales. (No commission is earned for the rental of apartments.) Shopping allowance—$1,000 (new employees only). Health insurance coverage—individual. Sick days—two per quarter. Personal days—five per year.

Real Estate Agent Duties

Sell Homes

Help clients find and purchase a home (from the list provided) that is compatible with their family size, income level, and tastes. Married couples **must** buy a home; single people may purchase homes if they wish. The home must have at least one bedroom for each person or married couple in the household. Monthly mortgage payments should not exceed 25 percent of a client's gross monthly income. More than one client may make an offer on a house. The seller (for this project, your teacher) can accept whichever offer he or she pleases—the first or the best offer.

Clients decide how much they want to offer for a home. The offer should be less than the listed selling price but not so low as to insult the seller. Normally, the real estate agent submits the offer to the seller in a written purchase agreement. If the seller does not accept the offer, the real estate agent writes up a different offer and tries again. To save time in this simulation, simply tell your teacher what the offer is and ask if it will be accepted before you write the purchase agreement.

Fill Out the Purchase Agreement

When an offer is accepted, complete Form A, as follows.

Number 1. List date, time, name of buyer(s), and address of the property. (Students can use their own address.) Only the items listed here will be left with the house. If the seller agreed to leave additional items, list them. (Sometimes, for example, the seller agrees to leave the stove and refrigerator.)

Number 2. Enter the purchase price and collect a minimum of $1,500 "earnest" money, so-called because it shows the seller that the buyer is serious ("earnest") about buying this house. Enter the balance due (purchase price less earnest money). The earnest money reserves the house for a set period while the buyer arranges financing for the remainder of the purchase price. The earnest money becomes part of the down payment when the sale is executed. If the buyer decides not to buy the house, the earnest money is forfeited.

Number 3. The agreement is binding only if the client can arrange appropriate financing. If the client cannot get a loan, the earnest money is returned. For this simulation, clients have five business days to apply for a loan. The loan must be approved within seven days of the signing date of the purchase agreement. Part of your job as real estate agent is to help buyers arrange for this loan. You can work with the loan officer to speed the process.

Number 4. Set a date for the closing (actual sale) to take place. On this day, the buyer and seller sign final papers, and the seller receives the balance due on the house. For this project, closing occurs on the first of the following month.

Number 5. The seller must maintain insurance on the house in the amount of the purchase price until closing. Enter the purchase price. The buyer must obtain a homeowner's insurance policy to take effect on the closing date before the bank will loan money for the purchase. Let clients know they will have to talk to the home insurance agent after the purchase agreement is completed.

Number 6. Make sure the buyer understands all terms and conditions stated here.

Number 7. Sign and date the purchase agreement. The real estate agent signs as a representative of Just 4 You Realty. Print names below signatures. At the bottom of the purchase agreement, paste a copy of the house listing. Cut it from the extra copy of the house listings. Once a house is purchased, take it off the market. It cannot be bought by anyone else.

Complete the Financing Worksheet

This worksheet (Form B) compares the costs to the buyer of borrowing at an 8 percent interest rate or at 7 percent interest plus two points (see sample on page 78). Points are sometimes called loan origination fees or loan discount fees. A point is equal to 1 percent of the loan amount. Charging two points means that the lending institution collects 2 percent of the loan amount in payment for the more favorable interest rate, here 7 percent. The purchase price and down payment are the same for both rates.

1. List the purchase price.
2. A minimum of 10 percent of the purchase price must be paid as a down payment. Remind clients that the down payment money can come from their savings account or from the cash value of their life insurance policy. The earnest money that was collected with the purchase agreement is also applied to the down payment.
3. Determine the amount financed by subtracting the down payment from the purchase price.
4. Determine the cost of two points and apply that figure to the 7 percent loan.
5. Complete the payment chart. Determine the monthly payment by using the monthly payment table, a business calculator, a computer, or a formula. (You should have a copy of the table and calculation instructions. Ask your teacher which method you should use.)
Total monthly payments = monthly payment × number of payments
Total interest paid = total monthly payments − amount financed
Total amount paid = total monthly payment + total down payment
+ point money (if any)
6. Calculate 25 percent of your client's gross monthly income. Your client's maximum monthly mortgage payment cannot be greater than this amount.
7. Help your clients choose a payment option that will fit their budget.
8. Enter the date of loan approval and your commission.

Complete the Statement of Account and Collect Closing Costs

Complete Form C. You know the real property costs. The other closing costs, which the real estate agent collects, must be added.

1. Appraisal: This gives the value and a detailed description of the property. Banks use the appraisal to determine how much money they can loan on a house. Cost of appraisal: $250.
2. Abstract of Title: This legal documentation passes the title through the legal system to the new owner. It is required with every real estate purchase. A record of this process is kept at the county courthouse or local land records office. Cost of abstract of title: $125.
3. Lawyer's Opinion: A lawyer performs a title search to make sure that the buyer can get clear title to the property—that is, that no one else has a claim of ownership against it. Cost of lawyer's opinion: $300.

4. Total Due: Once the loan has been approved and closing costs computed, collect for the remainder of the down payment, the amount financed, and the closing costs. The Loan Officer will give clients a check made out to both the buyer and the Just 4 You Trust Fund.

Complete the Accounts Receivable Cards

1. Enter Amount Due: Create a separate accounts receivable card for each sale. Enter the purchase price and the costs of the appraisal, abstract of title, and lawyer's opinion for each home buyer.
2. Enter Amount Paid: As you collect each check, enter the amount of the payment and the check number on the appropriate accounts receivable card and compute the new balance. (The total earnest money would be entered immediately as a payment when you create an accounts receivable card, because you would already have the buyer's first check in hand.)

Enter All Transactions in the Business Checking Ledger

1. Enter deposits daily:
   - Fill out a business checking deposit slip for all checks received that day.
   - Record the deposit in the checking ledger.
   - Be sure that all checks are made out to both the buyer and Just 4 You Realty and are endorsed by both parties.
   - Staple deposit slip and checks together and give to Bank Account Manager or leave in deposit drop box.
2. Reimburse Budget Plus, Inc.—Payroll Account:
   - Make out a check for 85 percent of the daily deposit.
   - Record the check in the checking ledger.
   - Give the check to the Payroll Clerk.
3. Reimburse Seller (teacher) 85% of deposit.

Complete the Commission Statement

- After you complete a purchase agreement, record the purchase price on the Commission Statement.
- Once all students interested in purchasing a home have done so, total the sales to compute the commission. Commission = Amount of Sales × Commission Rate, or 6 percent of sales.
- Give the Commission Statement to the Payroll Clerk so your commission is included in your next paycheck.

Just 4 You Realty
House Listings

3BR, 2BA Cape, custom kitchen, hardwood floors, 2 fireplaces, $146,900

4BR Colonial, 2.5BA, FR, 6 acres, near schools & Portland, reduced to $144,900

Briarwood Estates, 8 room Gambrel, attached garage, fireplace, fenced backyard, $143,500

Easy access, family neighborhood, spacious 4BR, 2BA Gambrel, 2-car garage, $139,900

3BR, 1.5 BA, oak kitchen, open floor plan, 2-car garage, $139,900

Traditional expanded 3BR Cape, 3/4 acre, giant private backyard, lg new office, DR, eat-in kitchen, $132,900

Colonial, 4BR, 2BA, convenient elegance priced to sell, $129,900

4BR, 1.5BA Ranch w/ finished daylight basement and 2-car garage. In- town location on quiet cul-de-sac, 1.2-acre lot, $129,900

4BR Split, 1.5BA, last on dead end, in-ground pool, lg lot, 2-car garage, $129,000

3BR raised Ranch on cul-de-sac, huge yard, deck, brick patio, finished basement, hardwood floors, in great condition, $126,000

Family home in family neighborhood, 3–4BR, 1 3/4 BA, tri-level, 2-car garage, lg yard, $126,000

Contemporary saltbox, 4BR, 2BA, 3-acre private lot, great location, $122,500

Big Cape, 4BR, 2BA, like new, great area, $121,900

Ranch w/daylight basement, 3BR, lg kitchen w/breakfast bar, lg FR, BA w/heat lamps, new forced hot-water heat, central vacuum, sliders onto lg wrap-around deck to view spa-

cious 2.8 acres w/arbor and flower gardens. Many extras, must see, $120,000

New listing: 5-yr-old dormer Cape, 3–4BR, 1 3/4 BA, full basement, wooded 1/2-acre at dead end, abuts executive subdivision, $119,900

3BR Ranch, garage, new furnace, roof, windows, $119,000

3BR full-dormered Cape on 1 + acre, rear deck, backyard, $116,900

Peaceful setting, popular neighborhood, expandable 2BR, fireplace, hardwood, in-ground pool, $114,900

3BR, 2BA Cape, 2-car garage, hardwood, tile, $114,900

Large 4BR, 2BA Painted lady, $114,900

4BR, convenient and private, lg yard, wood/coal stove, home warranty, $113,111

3BR, 1BA w/sun room, LR/w fireplace, 1-car garage, $110,000

Charming 3BR Colonial, hardwood floors, china closet. Move right in. $109,900

Cape w/charm, porch, fireplace, DR, garage, hardwood, $109,900

26×32 dormered split foyer, .5-acre lot, established neighborhood, $109,900

3BR, 2BA, FR w/fireplace, fenced yard, $109,000

3BR, hardwood floors, new bath & kitchen, 2 lg decks, above-ground pool, full basement, dead-end street, $105,000

Contemporary Ranch w/hardwood & tile, lg deck & yard, $102,500

3BR, 1BA, immaculate, updated home, $102,430

3BR Cape, FR, hardwood floors, $99,900

Cozy 2BR, lg LR, fireplace, hardwood floors, deck, 1-car garage, room for expansion, $99,500

3BR Ranch, lg corner lot, daylight basement, forced hot water/oil, in excellent move-in condition, $99,000

Immaculate 3–4BR on 1 acre, deck, formal DR, large FR, $95,000

New Cape on private 3.65-acre lot, 10-year warranty, $91,500

3BR Ranch w/finished addition, new roof, siding & insulation, hardwood/tile floors, $89,900

24×40 3BR Ranch w/daylight basement, large private, sunny lot, $88,500

5 rooms, 3BR, hardwood floors, dead-end street, 1-year warranty, $85,000

3BR Ranch on 1 +-acre lot in family neighborhood, $82,900

New listing: 2BR, 1BA, expandable 2nd level, 2.75-acre lot, $79,900

Walk downtown from this 2BR bungalow; public water/sewer, $69,900

2BR, 1BA, ceramic floors in kitchen/bath, 1st-floor laundry possible, $53,750

2BR, 1BA, newly remodeled and updated, new roof, furnace, $45,000

2BR, 1BA new furnace and water heater, partially remodeled, $47,500

BA = bathroom
BR = bedroom
DR = dining room
FR = family room
LR = living room

Form A—Real Estate Agent/Purchase Agreement form

Just 4 You Realty
Residential Real Estate Purchase Agreement

1. On this _____ day of _____, _____ at _____ A.M./P.M. Just 4 You Realty (seller) agrees to sell and convey to _____ (buyer) the following property located at _____ in Ward County, Iowa, including all fixtures such as lighting, heating, plumbing, outdoor plantings, window covering and hardware, central air-conditioning units and ducting, attached awnings, antennas, attached mirrors, built-in kitchen appliances, wall-to-wall carpeting, water softener, mailbox, storm windows and doors, garage-door openers, and _____.

2. The buyer agrees to pay the seller the sum of $_____ as follows: $_____ will accompany this offer as earnest money to be held by Just 4 You Realty pending final approval of all conditions and terms by both parties. The Balance of $_____ will be paid by cashier's check to Just 4 You Trust Fund and delivered to seller at closing.

3. This offer is made subject to buyer obtaining financing. The buyer shall make application for financing within _____ business days of the date of this agreement. Written confirmation of approved financing will be made on or before _____.

4. Possession and closing date shall be on or before _____.

5. The seller will maintain insurance on the described property in the amount of $_____ until the date of closing, at which time the buyer will become responsible for insurance on the property.

6. All real estate taxes shall be prorated between the buyer and the seller as of the date of closing. The seller will pay any expenses necessary to provide merchantable title, free and clear of encumbrances such as back taxes, liens, and assessments unless otherwise noted and agreed upon. The buyer's expenses shall include any loan fees, surveying costs, abstract recording fees, and credit searches. Seller agrees to maintain premises in present condition with the exception of normal wear and tear. Termite inspection shall be the expense of the seller, if required by the buyer's lending institution. It shall be the seller's responsibility and expense to terminate the lease of any existing tenants.

7. Signature of Seller _____ Signature of Buyer _____

   Name_____ Name _____
   Just 4 You Realty

   Date _____ S.S. # _____

   Name _____

   S.S. # _____

   Date _____

Paste copy of house listing here.

Teaching Consumer Concepts

Form B—Real Estate Agent/Financing Worksheet form

Just 4 You Realty
Financing Worksheet

	8%	7%
1. Purchase Price	_____	_____
2. Down Payment (10% of Purchase Price)	_____	_____
3. Amount Financed	_____	_____
4. Amount of 2 Points		_____
5.		

	PAYMENT CHART					
	8%			7%		
	15 years	20 years	30 years	15 years	20 years	30 years
Number of Payments	180	240	360	180	240	360
Monthly Payment						
Total Monthly Payments						
Total Interest Paid						
Down Payment						
Points						
TOTAL AMOUNT PAID						

6. Financing Available:
   Annual Income $ _____
   Monthly Income $ _____
   25% of Monthly Income $ _____
8. Date Loan Approved _____

7. Payment Schedule Chosen:
   Rate _____
   Years to Repay _____
   Monthly Payment $ _____
   Commission Earned $ _____

Form B—Real Estate Agent/Statement of Account form

Just 4 You Realty
Statement of Account

Date _____

Name _____ (Buyer)

Property Address _____

Bedrooms _____   # Baths _____   Date of Closing _____

Real Property Costs:	**Amount**	**Date paid**
Purchase price	_____	_____
Earnest money	_____	_____
Balance due on purchase price	_____	_____
Down payment (less earnest money)	_____	_____
Amount financed	_____	_____
Other closing costs:		
Appraisal	_____	_____
Abstract of title	_____	_____
Lawyer's opinion	_____	_____
Total Due	_____	_____

Teaching Consumer Concepts

Leasing Agent Duties

Rent Apartments

Help single clients find an apartment from the listings provided that is compatible with their lifestyle and income level. (Married couples must purchase a house.) Once you have rented a unit, take it off the market. Your clients must follow these guidelines in choosing an apartment:

1. Monthly rent should not exceed 25 percent of a renter's gross monthly income. Assume an annual income of $24,000 for clients who work on commission.
2. Single adults with no children may share an apartment and the expenses for that apartment. However, each single adult must have his or her own bedroom.
3. Single adults with children may not share an apartment with other adults. Encourage these families to provide one bedroom per person. If necessary, you may allow two children per bedroom to help renters meet the 25 percent guideline.

Complete the Lease Agreement (Form D)

Number 1. Enter the date and the name of the renter (lessee). If there is more than one renter, enter names as follows: John A. Smith and Kevin R. Green.

Number 2. Enter the renter's current address (the address the customer has used on other forms).

Number 3. The lease begins the first of the following month.

Number 4. Rent is due on the first day of every month.

Number 5. Read through and explain each condition to your client. List the number of adults renting the apartment. Check the appropriate box for pets. List any utilities that Budget Plus Development Corp. provides or enter "none."

Number 6. Adult renters and the apartment manager must sign and date the lease. At the bottom of the lease agreement, paste a copy of the apartment advertisement. Cut it from the second copy of the apartment rentals.

Complete the Deposit Summary/Receipt (Form E)

Number 1. Enter the renter's name, the address of the property he/she is renting, and the date.

Number 2. Enter the security deposit amount. (The security deposit equals one month's rent.) This one-time expense will be returned in full when the renter moves out if the apartment suffers no damage beyond normal wear and tear. However, the cost of damage beyond normal wear and tear is deducted from the security deposit. If damage costs exceed the security deposit, the renter must make up the difference or the situation might wind up in court.

Number 3. A key deposit of $50 is collected to cover the cost of lost, mislaid, or stolen keys. This one-time expense will be returned if the keys are returned when the renter moves out.

Number 4. Add the security deposit and the key deposit to get the total deposit due.

Number 5. Tell renters to list the rent, the amount that is due each month, on their cash flow summary. They do not need to include the security deposit and key deposit on the cash flow summary because these expenses will be returned if the renter takes care of the apartment.

Number 6. Have renters make their checks payable to Budget Plus Development Corp. for the total amount due.

Number 7. Complete this section after you receive a check for the total amount due.

Complete the Accounts Receivable Cards

Create a separate accounts receivable card for each renter. Unmarried adults sharing an apartment should be listed on separate Accounts Receivable cards, with the amount due apportioned equally to each renter.

1. Enter Amount Due: Enter the total of the monthly rent, security deposit, and key deposit as the first amount due for each renter. Subsequent payments will be for the monthly rent only.
2. Enter Amount Paid: As you collect each check, enter the amount of the payment on the appropriate accounts receivable card and compute the new balance.

Enter All Transactions in the Business Checking Ledger

1. Enter deposits daily:
   - Fill out a business checking deposit slip.
   - Record the total deposit in the checking ledger.
   - Be sure that all checks are endorsed "For deposit only to the account of Budget Plus Development Corp."
   - Staple deposit slip and checks together and give to Bank Account Manager or leave in deposit drop box.
2. Reimburse Budget Plus, Inc.—Payroll Account:
   - Make out a check for 80 percent of the daily deposit.
   - Record the check in the checking ledger.
   - Give the check to the Payroll Clerk.

Budget Plus Development Corp.
Apartment Rentals

Furnished Apartments

1BR, $120/wk, all utilities included + security deposit

1BR, LR, kitchen, all amenities, W/D, sunny, private. $515/mo. + utilities, security deposit

2BR, all utilities, no pets. Avail. till 6/15, $100/wk.

Clean, quiet, newly decorated, no pets, 3rd floor, 2 rooms & bath, parking, $95/wk + utilities, security deposit

Unfurnished Apartments
(monthly rates)

One Bedroom

1BR basement unit, all utilities, $320, no dogs

1BR, 2nd floor, just remodeled, $350 w/parking

1BR, hardwood floors, gas heat, laundry, $360, HW included

Cozy 1BR, hardwood floors, $375, heat & HW included

Heated, 1BR, first floor, remodeled bldg., security deposit, references/no pets, $390

Gracious LR, DR, 1BR, heat, HW, laundry, elevator, NS, no pets, $425, security deposit

SUNNY Victorian 1 BR, $425/mo., includes heat, HW, hardwood floors

1 or 2BR, recently renovated, very clean, $475 + utilities, security deposit

1BR newly renovated, off-street parking, private deck, $475, NS, no pets

Very attractive 1BR, hardwood floors, lg window, new paint, quiet secure bldg, parking, W/D, $500

Pleasant 1BR, hardwood floors, coin-op W/D, parking, no pets, heated, $500/mo.

1BR in quiet & secure house, $525, includes all utilities, non-smoker

1BR in historic brick, hardwood floors, nice features, no pets, laundry, $550 includes all utilities

1BR off-street parking, $685 includes all utilities + cable

Lg sunny 1BR, garden, parking, lg yard, $950 + utilities

Two Bedrooms

2BR, hardwood floors, $475/mo. includes heat & HW

Convenient 2BR, parking, $475, heated

SPACIOUS 2BR, lg yard, great location, W/D hookup, heated, $550

2BR, $575, includes heat; security deposit & references required, no pets

Lg 2BR, quiet building, new deck, laundry, off-street parking, $600 heated

SUNNY, QUIET 2BR, parking, storage, $625 + utilities, no pets

Spacious, quiet 2BR, heat & HW included, $650, no dogs

1st floor 2BR, includes all utilities, coin-op laundry, $650 + security deposit and references, pets ok

2BR, $675 laundry, parking, no dogs or smokers

1st floor, hardwood floors, 2BR, lg rooms, fireplace, lease, security deposit, no pets, $675 + utilities

Beautiful sunny 2BR w/water views, deck, 2 lofts, parking, heated, $750, cats ok

Three Bedrooms

Lg 3BR, laundry, parking, $500 + utilities

Lg 3BR, DR, newly decorated, W/D, parking, $625, lease, security deposit

Sunny 3BR, heated, new W/W, parking, $675/mo., security deposit

Lg 3BR, 1st floor, hardwood floors, parking, $695 + utilities and security deposit

3BR, W/W, off-street parking, on-site laundry, no pets, $725 + security deposit and utilities

3BR, 3 story, eat-in kitchen, yard, parking, storage, $750

HW = hot water
NS = no smoking
W/D = washer/dryer
W/W = wall-to-wall carpeting
BR = bedroom
LR = living room
DR = dining room

Budget Plus Development Corp.
Apartment Lease Agreement

1. On this _____ day of _____, _____, Budget Plus Development Corp. (Lessor) and _____ (Lessee) enter into this monthly rental agreement.

2. Budget Plus Development Corp. agrees to lease the apartment located at _____ _____ to the lessee for the purposes of a primary residence.

3. This will be a tenancy from month to month, commencing on the _____ day of _____, _____.

4. In return, the lessee agrees to pay consideration of $_____ per month, payable in advance but due no later than the _____ of each month.

5. Conditions:
   a. The agreed-upon premises shall be occupied by no more than _____ adults and children.
   b. Pets are/are not allowed on the premises.
   c. Utilities will be the responsibility of the lessee, except for _____ _____, which shall be paid for by Budget Plus Development Corp.
   d. Lessee shall be responsible for any damage caused by family or guests' negligence.
   e. Lessee shall keep and maintain the premises in a clean and sanitary condition. A security deposit of one month's rent shall be kept until termination of the lease. At that time, an inspection of the premises will be conducted and deductions will be made for damage beyond normal wear and tear. Any remaining security deposit will be returned to the lessee within a period of three (3) weeks.
   f. Lawn care and snow removal shall be the responsibility of Budget Plus Development Corp.
   g. Subletting is not permitted without the prior written consent of the lessor.
   h. Termination of the lease will take place after either party gives thirty (30) days notice or in the event of nonpayment of timely rent, not less than three (3) days after lessee receives written notice of termination of the lease agreement.

6. Signatures:

_____
Budget Plus Development Corp. Manager

_____ lessee #1

_____ date

_____ lessee #2

_____ date

_____
date

_____ lessee #3

_____ date

Paste Apartment Advertisement Here

Teaching Consumer Concepts

Budget Plus Development Corp.
Deposit Summary/Receipt

1. Tenant's Name _____ Date _____

   Address _____

2. Security Deposit $ _____

3. Key Deposit $ _____

4. Total Deposit $ _____

5. 1st Month's Rent $ _____

6. Total Due (total deposits + 1st month's rent) $ _____

7. Date Paid _____ Check Number _____

   Approved by _____

Teaching Consumer Concepts

Insurance Agent—Home

Job Description: Sells property insurance to renters and home owners. Explains various types of coverage and advises clients on ways to cut their insurance costs. Computes the cost of insurance coverage.

Education Requirements: Minimum of two years of post-secondary education and some previous sales experience.

Benefits: Earnings are based on salary plus commissions. Base salary— $18,000 per year, plus 20 percent commission on insurance premiums. Health insurance coverage provided—individual. Shopping allowance—$1,000 (new employees only). Sick days—two per quarter. Personal days—five per year.

Duties

Explain Types of Coverage

Two types of standard property coverage are available to your clients.

Form HO-3 provides home owners with comprehensive coverage on their house for all risks except wear and tear, earthquake, flood, termites, dry rot, rodent infestation, and war. Contents are covered for the same perils as in HO-4.

Form HO-4 provides renters with broad coverage on the contents of their rental units in the event of damage or loss from fire, lightning, windstorm, hail, theft, glass breakage, explosion, smoke, aircraft, vehicles, vandalism, riot, collapse, falling objects, freezing, and power surges.

Two important types of optional coverage are also available to your clients.

Replacement cost endorsement is an option that clients can add to their personal property coverage for an additional premium. This option is well worth the extra money because it reimburses policy holders for the replacement cost of an item (less the deductible) regardless of the item's age. For example, if your six-year-old refrigerator is hit by lightning, a policy without a replacement cost endorsement would depreciate the refrigerator's value by 60 percent based on a 10-year lifetime. With a replacement cost endorsement, however, you would get almost full reimbursement.

without replacement	with replacement
cost endorsement	cost endorsement

$800 Cost to replace
    refrigerator
−$480 Depreciation ($800 × 60%)
    $320 Actual cash value
−$100 Deductible
    $220 Insurance payout

$800 Cost to replace
    refrigerator
−$100 Deductible
    $700 Insurance payout

A replacement cost endorsement will be sold with every policy in this project.

Waterbed liability is an option that renters may want to add to their personal property coverage. This option protects renters from liability claims that may arise if their waterbed springs a leak and causes damage to the building where they are renting.

Complete the Home Owner's/Renter's Insurance Application (Form A)

1. Complete the applicant information section. The effective date is the date of possession (see the purchase agreement or lease). The expiration date is one year later. The mortgagee is the bank holding the loan (Big Bucks Savings Bank).
2. Complete the coverage section:
   - Check the form of coverage requested. Use form HO-3 for home owners. Use form HO-4 for apartment renters; it covers contents and liability, but not the building.
   - Use table 1 to determine coverage amounts. For home owners, let coverage A (Dwelling) equal the purchase price of the house. For renters, enter "NA" (not applicable) for coverage A and B. To determine the amount of coverage C, assume that renters' personal property is worth 80 percent of their annual gross income, unless this amount is less than the minimum value of $15,000. (Assume the gross income for commissioned customers is $24,000.) Round to the nearest amount shown on the renter's insurance chart.
   - Choose a deductible of $100 or $250.
   - Check the boxes for additional endorsements. Home owners purchase replacement cost endorsement. Renters with waterbeds may opt to purchase waterbed endorsement.
3. Complete the dwelling information:
   - Big Bucks has a good fire department—protection class 3.
   - Answer "yes" to the smoke alarm question.
   - This house is the primary residence.
   - Answer "no" to the listed questions.

4. Complete the premiums section:
   - Find the base premium in table 2, Annual Rates.
   - If a $250 deductible is chosen, determine the amount of the discount on the premium.
   - Add the charge for replacement cost endorsement and for waterbed endorsement, if applicable.
   - Find the total. Collect this amount from the applicant.
5. Complete the binder, sign the application, and have the applicant sign. The insurance is now in force.

Complete the Accounts Receivable Card

Create a separate accounts receivable card for each policy sold.
1. Enter Amount Due: For each policy, enter the annual premium due.
2. Enter Amount Paid: As you collect each check, enter the amount of the payment and the check number on the appropriate accounts receivable card and compute the new balance.

Enter All Transactions in the Business Checking Ledger

1. Enter deposits daily.
   - Fill out a business checking deposit slip for all checks received that day.
   - Record the total deposit in the checking ledger.
   - Be sure all checks are endorsed "For deposit only to the account of Country Insurance Agency."
   - Staple deposit slip and checks together and give to Bank Account Manager or leave in deposit drop box.
2. Reimburse Budget Plus, Inc.—Payroll Account:
   - Make out a check for 80 percent of the daily deposit.
   - Record the check in the checking ledger.
   - Give the check to the Payroll Clerk.

Complete the Commission Statement

- After you sell a policy, record the sale price on the Commission Statement.
- When all students in the simulation have purchased home/renter's insurance and life insurance, total the annual premiums to compute your commission. Commission = Amount of Annual Premiums × Commission Rate, or 20 percent of home owner's and renter's insurance premiums.
- Give the Commission Statement to the Payroll Clerk so your commission will be included in your next paycheck.

Table 1. Coverage Amounts

Type of Coverage	HO-3 (Home owners)	HO-4 (Renters)
A. **Dwelling**—covers the house itself, decks, porches, attached garages.	Purchase price $40,000 minimum	NA
B. **Other Structures**—covers detached garages, permanent sheds, antennas; normally does not cover satellite dishes or pools.	10% of amount "A"	NA
C. **Personal Property**—covers contents such as furniture, clothing, food, appliances, lawnmowers, tools, etc.	50% of amount "A"	Minimum of $15,000
D. **Loss of Use**—covers additional living expenses (e.g., motels, eating out) when home is uninhabitable after a covered loss.	20% of amount "A"	40% of amount "C"
E. **Liability**—pays medical bills of others injured while on your property if the injury is your fault.	$100,000	$100,000
F. **Medical Payments**—pays medical bills of others injured on your property, even if you are not at fault.	$1,000	$1,000

Endorsements
Replacement cost on contents: $20 flat fee
Waterbed liability: $15 flat fee

Table 2. Annual Rates

Home owner's Insurance   HO-3 $100 Deductible*

Amount of Coverage on Dwelling**	Protection Class			
	1–6	7–8	9	10
$40,000	$201	$211	$290	$325
45,000	209	219	302	338
50,000	214	225	310	347
55,000	232	243	335	375
60,000	243	255	352	394
65,000	260	273	377	423
70,000	272	285	394	442
75,000	292	306	424	476
80,000	306	321	444	498
85,000	335	351	486	546
90,000	354	371	514	577
95,000	373	391	542	609
100,000	392	411	570	640
Add for each additional $5,000	20	21	28	32

*For $250 Deductibles, take 85% of base premium and round to nearest dollar.
**All other coverage included in base premium.

Renter's Insurance   HO-4 $100 Deductible*

Amount of Coverage on Contents**	Protection Class			
	1–6	7–8	9	10
$15,000	$93	$96	$133	$150
16,000	96	99	138	155
17,000	98	102	142	160
18,000	101	105	146	165
19,000	104	108	151	170
20,000	107	111	155	174
25,000	122	127	176	199
30,000	136	143	198	223
Add for each additional $5,000	16	16	22	25

*For $250 Deductibles, take 85% of base premium and round to nearest dollar.
**All other coverage included in base premium.

Teaching Consumer Concepts

Form A—Insurance Agent—Home/Insurance Application form

Home Owner/Renter Insurance Application

Name _____ Date _____

Address _____ Phone _____

City, State, Zip _____

Effective Date _____ Expiration Date _____

Mortgagee _____

Coverage: Check one _____ HO-3 _____ HO-4

Amounts of Coverage:

A. Dwelling _____ Deductible amount _____

B. Other structures _____ Endorsements:

C. Personal property _____ Replacement cost _____

D. Loss of use _____ Waterbed liability _____

E. Liability _____

F. Medical Payments _____

Dwelling Information: Protection class: _____

Smoke alarms on every floor: _____ Yes _____ No

Check one: _____ Primary residence _____ Seasonal residence

1. Any business conducted on premises? _____ Yes _____ No

2. Any full-time employees of the residence? _____ Yes _____ No

3. Any swimming pools on premises? _____ Yes _____ No

    If yes, _____ In-ground _____ Aboveground

4. Any wood/coal-burning stove on premises? _____ Yes _____ No

5. Any solar heating on premises? _____ Yes _____ No

6. Any insurance canceled within last three years? _____ Yes _____ No

    If yes, explain below:

Premiums:

    Base premium _____

    Discount for higher deductible _____

    Adjusted base premium _____

    Optional endorsements:

       Replacement cost _____

       Waterbed liability _____

    Total Annual Premium (paid with application) _____

Binder of Coverage:

_____ Coverage is bound as of _____ (effective date) at _____ A.M./P.M.

Can be canceled by the applicant with written notice or canceled by the company according to the procedures outlined in the policy.

    I have read the above application. To the best of my knowledge all statements made are accurate and true.

Applicant's Signature: _____

Agent's Signature: _____

Loan Officer

Job Description: Helps customers fill out applications for home and car loans. Approves or denies loan applications and issues checks for approved loan amounts. Computes interest and monthly loan payments. Accepts loan payments. Prepares end-of-year interest payment statements.

Education Requirements: Undergraduate degree in business administration, with a major in finance or banking services. Participation in banking seminars and some experience working in the bank is beneficial.

Benefits: Starting salary—$26,000. Shopping allowance—$1,000 (new employees only). Health insurance coverage provided—individual. Sick days—two per quarter. Personal days—five per year.

Duties

Process Car Loan Applications (Form A).

Each student in the simulation must purchase a car. Most will need a loan for this purchase.

1. Complete the loan application
   - Fill out the information on the buyer and, if applicable, on the co-buyer.
   - See Car Dealer for vehicle description (contained in the purchase agreement or Car Dealer's listings).
   - Determine the loan amount. Customers can borrow up to 80 percent of the purchase price (see the Motor Vehicle Purchase Agreement). Ask the customer how much is needed.
   - Complete the Truth in Lending Disclosures and Payment Schedule in the following order:
     - Amount Financed (amount of loan).
     - Payments Start On (the month the vehicle is purchased).
     - Number of Years to pay off the loan—depends on the age of the vehicle. A car that is one to three years old takes a four-year loan; four to five years old takes a three-year loan; and six or more years old takes a two-year loan. Customers may choose shorter loan periods if they wish.

- Number of Payments equals the number of loan years × 12.
- Monthly Payment can be calculated using a formula, the monthly payment table, a business calculator, or a computer. (You should have a copy of the table and calculation instructions. Ask your teacher which method you should use.)
- Total of Payments
  (Number of Payments × Monthly Payment).
- Finance Charge, or interest paid
  (Total of Payments – Amount Financed).
- Total Cost of Vehicle—see purchase agreement
  (Purchase Price + Sales Tax + Title Fee + Finance Charge).
- Complete the Itemization of Amount Financed:
  - Total Cash Price = Purchase Price + Sales Tax + Title Fee.
  - Total Down Payment = Cash Price − Amount Financed.
  - Trade-in Allowance = $1,500.
  - Cash Balance Down = Total Down Payment − Trade-in Allowance.
- Make sure buyers read the loan application; answer any questions they have, and have them sign the application.

2. Make out check for the loan amount, payable to the borrower *and* Colden's Cool Cars. The borrower endorses the check at the Car Dealer's office using a nonrestrictive endorsement. The Car Dealer endorses the check with a restrictive endorsement ("for deposit only") and deposits it in Colden's Cool Cars business checking account.

3. Complete a Bank Authorization Form (Form B) and turn it in with a deposit slip. The Bank Account Manager will automatically deduct the monthly payment from the client's account on the same day each month. Remind borrowers to deduct this payment from their check register.

Complete the Accounts Receivable Cards

Create a separate accounts receivable card for each borrower.

1. At the top of the card, record the total amount of the loan.
2. Enter Amount Due: For each borrower, enter the amount of the monthly payment.
3. Enter Amount Paid: As you collect each check, enter the amount of the payment and the check number on the appropriate accounts receivable card. For car loans, compute the new balance. For real estate loans, compute the new balance if you have amortized the loan for a one-year period; if not, leave the new balance column blank.

Enter All Transactions in the Business Checking Ledger

1. Enter deposits daily:
   - Fill out a business checking deposit slip for all checks received that day.
   - Record the total deposit on the checking ledger.
   - Be sure that all checks are endorsed "For deposit only to the account of Big Bucks Savings Bank."
   - Staple deposit slip and checks together and give to Bank Account Manager or leave in deposit drop box.
2. Reimburse Budget Plus, Inc.—Payroll Account:
   - Make out a check for 5 percent of the daily deposit. (Most employees reimburse the Payroll Clerk 80 percent. The Loan Officer does not because most of the money collected is used to replenish the loan account.)
   - Record the check in the checking ledger.
   - Give the check to the Payroll Clerk.

Process Real Estate Loan Applications (Form C).

All married couples must purchase a home; single people may purchase homes if they want to.

1. Meet with the real estate agent to determine whether the applicant meets the criteria for loan approval:
   - The amount of the loan can be no more than 90 percent of the purchase price.
   - The monthly payment cannot exceed 25 percent of the applicant's projected gross *monthly* income. For commissioned employees, assume an annual income of $24,000. Check real estate agent's Financing Worksheet for this client to determine which payment plan (interest rate, number of years) would fit client's budget.
2. Fill out the loan application.
   - Type of Mortgage—the loan is a conventional. Make sure the real estate agent computed the loan payment correctly. (Use a formula, monthly payment table, business calculator, or computer to calculate the payment. You should have a copy of the table and calculation instructions. Ask your teacher which method you should use.)
   - Property Information:
     - Purpose of Loan—to purchase.
     - Property Use—primary residence.
     - Source of Down Payment—savings or cash value of life insurance.
     - Real Estate Taxes—see County Treasurer to determine this tax amount.

Teaching Consumer Concepts

- Financial Statement—go over this information with the borrower. Assets are things you own; liabilities are things you owe.
  - Make sure information is current.
  - Under Assets, reduce cash value of life insurance by any amount the applicant has borrowed from it for the real estate down payment.
  - Under Assets, use the purchase price for the market value of real estate and the cash value of cars. However, do not list the real estate borrower hopes to buy if this loan is approved— the borrower does not own the real estate yet.
  - Under Liabilities, do not list the mortgage being applied for, because it has not yet been approved. Do list any car loans that have been approved.
- Have the buyer (and co-buyer) read through the application and sign it.
3. Figure and collect closing costs (at bottom of Form C).
   - Charge 1 point only if using the 8 percent interest rate (1 point = 1 percent of amount of loan.
   - Collect $50 for credit record search.

Make Out Check for the Loan Amount

Make check payable to the Borrower *and* Just 4 You Realty. Borrower endorses the check at the real estate agent's office using a nonrestrictive endorsement. The real estate agent endorses it using a restrictive endorsement ("for deposit only") and deposits it in the Just 4 You business checking account.

Collect the First Month's Payment. Record the Loan Transaction on the Borrower's Accounts Receivable Card and Enter All Transactions in the Business Checking Ledger.

See pages 94 and 95 in the car loans section and follow the same procedures.

Form A—Loan Officer/Car Loan Application form

Big Bucks Savings Bank, Inc.
Big Bucks, IA 00000

Car Loan Application

Buyer Information:

Name _____

Address _____

City, State, Zip _____

Phone _____

SS # _____

Co-buyer Information:

Name _____

Address _____

City, State, Zip _____

Phone _____

SS # _____

Vehicle Description: New _____   Used _____   Year _____   Make _____

   Model_____ Body type _____ VIN _____

Truth in Lending Disclosures:

Amount Financed	Annual Percentage Rate	Total of Payments	Finance Charge	Total Cost of Vehicle
	9%			

Payment Schedule: Payments start on _____ Number of payments _____

   Number of years _____   Amount of monthly payment _____

Security: You are giving security in this vehicle as collateral for the loan.

Late Charge: If any payment is not made within 10 days of its due date, a late charge of 5 percent of the amount due or $20.00, whichever is less, will be assessed.

Prepayment: Prepayment is allowed and will decrease the finance charge.

Itemization of Amount Financed: A. Total cash price (purchase price & taxes, etc.)   _____

   B. Less amount financed   _____

   C. Total down payment   _____

   D. Less trade-in allowance   _____

   E. Cash balance down   _____

Do not sign this application before you have read it completely. You are entitled to a copy of this paper. You may prepay at any time with no penalty. By signing this paper you are accepting all responsibility for making monthly payments.

Buyer's Signature   _____ Date _____

Co-buyer's Signature   _____ Date _____

Form B—Loan Officer/ Bank Authorization form

Bank Authorization Form

I, _____ , hereby authorize

_____(name of bank) to automatically deduct

$ _____ from my account number # _____ on the _____ day of every month. This authorization will be valid until further written notice is given to the bank.

   Signature _____

   Date _____

Teaching Consumer Concepts

Form C—Loan Officer/Real Estate Loan Application form

Big Bucks Savings Bank, Inc.
Big Bucks, IA 00000

Real Estate Loan Application

Borrower Information:

Name _____

Address _____

City, State, Zip _____

Phone_____

SS # _____ Age _____

Years of School _____ Marital Status __ M __ S __D

Name of Employer _____

Position _____ Years with company _____

Dependents _____ Ages_____

Co-borrower Information:

Name _____

Address _____

City, State, Zip _____

Phone # _____

SS # _____ Age _____

Years of School _____ Marital Status __ M __ S __ D

Name of Employer _____

Position _____ Years with company _____

Dependents _____ Ages _____

Type of Mortgage: _____ Conventional _____ VA _____ FHA _____ FMA _____ Other

   Amount of Loan _____ Interest Rate _____ Points _____

   # Years _____ # Payments _____ Payment Amount _____

Property Information: Purpose of Loan _____ Purchase _____ Refinance _____ Construction

   Property use _____ Primary residence _____ Investment _____ Secondary residence

   Property address _____

   Source of down payment _____

   Real estate taxes _____

Financial Statement:

Assets		Liabilities	
Checking account balance	_____	Mortgage balance	_____
Savings account balance	_____	Car loan #1	_____
Cash value of life insurance	_____	Car loan #2	_____
Market value of real estate	_____		
Cash value of car #1	_____		
Cash value of car #2	_____		
Other	_____		
Total Assets	_____	**Total Liabilities**	_____
		Net Worth	_____

Monthly Income: Buyer _____ Co-buyer _____

Total combined monthly income: _____

I agree that (1) the bank will hold first mortgage on this property, (2) the property will not be used for any illegal activities, (3) all statements made on this loan application are accurate and true to the best of my knowledge.

Signature of Borrower _____ Date _____

Signature of Co-borrower _____ Date _____

Closing Costs Payable to Big Bucks Savings Bank:

        _____ points $ _____

        Credit record search $ _____

Payroll Clerk

Job Description: Calculates net pay on the basis of allowances; marital status; hours worked (absenteeism); commissions earned; and withholdings for federal and state taxes, Social Security (FICA), Medicare, and family health insurance premiums. Issues payroll checks. Completes end-of-the-year W-2 forms.

Education Requirements: High school diploma and a minimum of one year of post-secondary education, with an emphasis in accounting.

Benefits: Starting salary—$19,600, with semiannual reviews. Health insurance coverage provided—individual. Shopping allowance—$1,000 (new employees only). Sick days—two per quarter. Personal days—five per year.

Duties

Complete Payroll Worksheet (Form A)

You can get the information you need about each employee's salary, commission rates, marital status, health insurance plan, and withholding status from the Personnel Manager.

1. Calculate gross pay. Paychecks are normally issued weekly (52 times a year), biweekly (every 2 weeks or 26 times a year), semi-monthly (twice a month or 24 times a year), or monthly (12 times a year). Budget Plus, Inc., pays employees semi-monthly. You will issue each employee two paychecks (one month's pay) during this simulation.
   - For employees whose gross pay is based on salary only, divide annual income by number of payments per year (e.g., $15,600 ÷ 24 = $650 Gross pay).
   - For employees whose gross pay is based on salary plus commissions, give them their monthly salary in their first paycheck and their monthly commission in their second paycheck. For example, suppose the Car Dealer's salary is $8,000 plus 1 percent of the first $50,000 in sales and 2 percent of sales over $50,000,

and his sales for this month are $65,000. Calculate his pay as follows:

1st paycheck: $8,000 ÷ 12 = $666.66 Gross Pay

2nd paycheck: $50,000 × 1% = $500 Commission, $15,000 × 2% = $300 Commission = $800 Monthly Commission

You cannot pay monthly commissions until you receive employees' Commission Statements, which will have the commission amount already computed. Check that the math is correct before you issue the check.

2. Calculate deductions.
   - Health insurance deduction: Take no paycheck deductions for employees who are on the Single Plan. Deduct $75 from each semimonthly paycheck for employees who are on the Family Plan. Check Employee Data Sheets in Personnel Manager's file.
   - Taxable pay is the portion of the employee's wages that is subject to state and federal withholding of taxes. Calculate as follows:
   Gross Pay − Health Insurance Deduction = Taxable Pay or Monthly Commission − Health Insurance Deduction = Taxable Pay
   - Federal withholding taxes pay for the costs of the national government, including such things as national defense, interstate highways, and upkeep of national parks.
     – Determine whether employee is single or married. Check W-4 forms in the Personnel Manager's files to determine the number of allowances claimed.
     – Look up semimonthly taxable income on the appropriate federal tax withholding table.
   - State withholding taxes are used to pay the costs of state government, including state parks, state roadways, and state schools.
     – Check W-4 form for the number of allowances claimed.
     – Look up semimonthly taxable income on the appropriate state tax withholding table.
   - Social Security (FICA) is used to provide supplemental income for retired, widowed, or disabled persons and income for minor children of workers who die. To calculate, take 6.2 percent of gross pay or monthly commissions.
   - Medicare tax is used to provide supplemental medical coverage for retired, widowed, or disabled persons and minor children of workers who die. To calculate, take 1.45 percent of gross pay or monthly commissions.

3. Calculate net pay (also called "take-home" pay). This is the amount the payroll check is made out for. Calculate as follows:
   Deductions = Health Insurance + Federal Tax + State Tax + FICA + Medicare
   Gross Pay − Deductions = Net Pay

Issue Payroll Checks

For each employee, transfer the information from the Payroll Worksheet to the top stub of the payroll check (Statement of Earnings and Deductions, Form B). Then make out the check (Form C) for the net pay amount. Each employee receives two checks and Statements of Earnings and Deductions during the simulation.

- 1st Check: The totals for the "year to date" column will be the same as the current amounts.
- 2nd Check: Enter only the amounts for the second check in the "current" column. Enter the combined total amounts for both checks in the year-to-date column.

Deposit Reimbursement Checks

Divisions of Budget Plus, Inc., reimburse the company for 80 percent of their daily sales, with a check made out to Budget Plus, Inc.— Payroll Account. As you receive these checks each day, endorse and deposit them.

Enter All Transactions in the Business Checking Ledger

- Enter payroll checks as issued.
- Enter reimbursement deposits daily.

Complete W-2 Forms (Form D).

At the simulation's end, use each employee's earnings for the month to project their earnings and withholdings for a year. Multiply this month's totals by 12, and then enter those figures on Form D, along with employee information.

Form A—Payroll Clerk/Worksheet form

Payroll Worksheet

Employee _____ Occupation _____

Salary _____ Commission Rate _____

Marital status _____ Number of allowances _____

1st Semimonthly check **2nd Semimonthly check**

Gross pay $ _____ Gross pay/commission $ _____

Health insurance deduction _____ Health insurance deduction _____

Taxable pay _____ Taxable pay _____

Federal withholding _____ Federal withholding _____

State withholding _____ State withholding _____

Social Security (FICA) _____ Social Security (FICA) _____

Medicare _____ Medicare _____

Net pay _____ Net pay _____

Form B—Payroll Clerk/Earnings Statement form

Budget Plus, Inc.

Employee _____

Statement of Earnings & Deductions

	Current	Year to Date
Gross pay/commission	_____	_____
Health insurance withholding	_____	_____
Taxable income	_____	_____
Federal tax withholding	_____	_____
State tax withholding	_____	_____
FICA	_____	_____
Medicare	_____	_____
Net pay	_____	_____

Pay period _____

SS # _____

Marital status _____

Allowances _____

Check date _____

Check number _____

Teaching Consumer Concepts

Form C—Payroll Clerk/Paycheck form

Budget Plus, Inc.
430 Consumer Lane
Big Bucks, IA 00000

Check No. _____

Date _____

Pay to the
Order of _____ $ _____

_____ Dollars

Big Bucks
Savings Bank

⑈071458⑈   138472011⑈   2428   **Budget Plus, Inc.**, *Payroll Clerk*

Form D—Payroll Clerk/IRS W-2 Statement form

a Control number	22222	Void ☐	For Official Use Only ► OMB No. 1545-0008	
b Employer's identification number			**1** Wages, tips, other compensation	**2** Federal income tax withheld
c Employer's name, address, and ZIP code			**3** Social security wages	**4** Social security tax withheld
			5 Medicare wages and tips	**6** Medicare tax withheld
			7 Social security tips	**8** Allocated tips
d Employee's social security number			**9** Advance EIC payment	**10** Dependent care benefits
e Employee's name (first, middle initial, last)			**11** Nonqualified plans	**12** Benefits included in box 1
			13 See Instrs. for box 13	**14** Other

	15 Statutory employee ☐	Deceased ☐	Pension plan ☐	Legal rep. ☐	Hshld. emp. ☐	Subtotal ☐	Deferred compensation ☐
f Employee's address and ZIP code							

16 State Employer's state I.D. No.	17 State wages, tips, etc.	18 State income tax	19 Locality name	20 Local wages, tips, etc.	21 Local income tax

Cat. No. 10134D

Department of the Treasury—Internal Revenue Service

W-2 Form **Wage and Tax Statement** **1998**

For Paperwork Reduction Act Notice, see separate instructions.

Copy A For Social Security Administration

Do NOT Cut or Separate Forms on This Page

Teaching Consumer Concepts

Personnel Manager

Job Description: Helps CEO select, train, and evaluate employees. Maintains employee records (applications, résumés, W-4's, etc.) and manages the group health insurance program. Fosters open communication between employees and managers.

Education Requirements: Undergraduate degree in business administration, with a major in industrial relations.

Benefits: Starting salary—$37,000, with annual reviews. Shopping allowance—$1,000 (new employees only). Health insurance coverage provided—individual. Sick days—two per quarter. Personal days—five per year.

Duties

Help Interview and Select Employees

For each job, create a file that contains information regarding the applicants.

- Hand out job applications (Form A) to potential employees, and schedule and help conduct interviews. Send out rejection letters (Form B) to unsuccessful applicants. Add applicant's name and address above the salutation ("Dear Applicant").

Maintain a File on Each Employee That Contains the Following:

1. Cover letter and résumé.
2. Completed job application (Form A). Check job applications to be sure they are neat, complete, and signed. If applicants have no job experience, they should write the word "none" across that section. They should answer "NA" to questions that are not applicable, so that you know they have not overlooked a question.
3. W-4 Form (Form C). Give each new employee a W-4 form and personal allowance worksheet to fill out. Check all completed W-4 forms to make sure they are correct.
   - Head of household status: The person must be a single parent to claim this allowance.

- Married with two incomes: Claim all allowances on the highest wage earner's form. Claim zero allowances on the second wage earner's form.
- Exemption: No one in this simulation is exempt from withholding taxes. To be exempt, you must not have paid taxes the previous year and your annual income must be less than $650.

4. Employee Data Sheet (Form D). Give each newly hired employee an employee data sheet to fill out, and review the completed form. Help employees choose the correct health insurance plan, as follows:
   - Employees with no children are on the Single Plan—the company pays the full premium, and no deductions are taken from the employee's paycheck.
   - Employees with children are on the Family Plan—the company pays employees' premiums, but employees must pay for their children's coverage, which costs $150 per month.
   - If employees are married with children, one parent selects the Family Plan so the children are covered. The other parent selects the Single Plan.

Train New Employees

You must understand all other positions so that you can help employees learn their jobs. Once you have trained employees, you periodically review their performance to see if they need any assistance. You will be evaluated, in part, on how well trained employees are.

Evaluate Students' Participation (Form E) in the Simulation

You must maintain a daily record of each student's participation in the course. Evaluate students' efficiency, politeness, attitude, cooperation, and effort in performing their jobs.

Keep Track of Absenteeism

Keep a daily record of employees' attendance (Form F) and let the Payroll Clerk know when someone takes more than two sick days per quarter (a two-week period for the purpose of this simulation). The additional time off will be deducted from paychecks.

Teaching Consumer Concepts

Form A—Personnel Manager/ Job Application form

Budget Plus, Inc.
430 Consumer Lane
Big Bucks, IA 00000-0000

Application for Employment

For Office Use only
Position: _____
Rate: _____
Date hired: _____

> Applicant will be considered for all positions, regardless of race, color, religion, sex, national origin, age, marital or veteran status, sexual orientation, the presence of a non-job-related medical condition or handicap, or any other legally protected status.

(PLEASE TYPE OR PRINT)   Date of Application: _____

Position(s) Applied For: _____

Name _____
           LAST   FIRST   MIDDLE

Address_____
        NUMBER   STREET   CITY   STATE   ZIP

Telephone (_____) _____ Social Security Number _____
       AREA CODE

Is there anything that would limit your ability to do the job? _____ yes _____ no

If yes, describe: _____

_____

Have you filed an application with Budget Plus, Inc., before? _____ yes _____ no

If yes, give date: _____

Have you ever been employed by Budget Plus, Inc.? _____ yes _____ no

If yes, give date and location: _____

Are you prevented from lawfully becoming employed in this country because of visa or immigration status? _____ yes _____ no
(Proof of citizenship or immigration status will be required upon employment)

On what date would you be available for work? _____

Are you available to work? _____ full-time _____ part-time _____ temporary

Are you on a layoff and subject to recall? _____ yes _____ no

Can you travel if a job requires it? _____ yes _____ no

Have you ever been convicted of a felony? _____ yes _____ no
(Conviction will not necessarily disqualify applicant from employment)

If yes, please explain: _____

_____

Veteran of the U.S. military service? _____ yes _____ no   If yes, branch _____

References

> Give name, address, and telephone number of three references who are not related to you and are not previous employers.
>
> _____
>
> _____
>
> _____

(continued)

Teaching Consumer Concepts

Form A—Personnel Manager/ Job Application form (continued)

Employment Experience

Start with your present or last job. Include military service assignments.

Name, Address, Type of business	From Mo	Yr	To Mo	Yr	Weekly Starting Salary	Weekly Ending Salary	Describe the work you did	Name of supervisor	Reason for leaving

Education

School	Name & Address	Course of Study	Years Attended From	To	Last year completed	Diploma/Degree
Elementary					5 6 7 8	
High School					9 10 11 12	
College					1 2 3 4	
Other						

Applicant's Statement

I certify that answers given herein are true and complete to the best of my knowledge.

I authorize investigations of all statements contained in this application for employment as may be necessary to make an employment decision.

In the event of employment, I understand that false or misleading information given in my application or interview(s) may result in discharge. I understand, also, that I am required to abide by all rules and regulations of the employer.

I understand that some positions could require a preemployment physical and drug test. (If required, you will be informed before you are offered a job.)

I also understand that some positions require an examination of driving records prior to employment.

Signature _____ Date _____

This application for employment shall be considered active for a period of time not to exceed six months. Any applicant wishing to be considered for employment beyond this period should inquire as to whether applications are being accepted at that time. The applicant understands that neither this document nor any offer of employment from the employer constitutes an employment contract unless a specific document to that effect is executed by the employer and employee in writing.

Budget Plus, Inc.
430 Consumer Lane
Big Bucks, IA 00000-0000

Dear Applicant:

We appreciate your recent application to Budget Plus, Inc. We wish to advise you that the position you applied for has been filled.

Thank you for the time and effort you put forth in seeking employment with us. We will keep your application on file for the next six months in case another position opens for which you are qualified. Please feel free to contact us regarding other opportunities for employment with Budget Plus, Inc.

We wish you success in your future endeavors.

Sincerely,

Personnel Manager

Form C—Personnel Manager/W-4 form

Form W-4 (1998)

Purpose. Complete Form W-4 so your employer can withhold the correct Federal income tax from your pay. Because your tax situation may change, you may want to refigure your withholding each year.

Exemption from withholding. If you are exempt, complete only lines 1, 2, 3, 4, and 7, and sign the form to validate it. Your exemption for 1998 expires February 16, 1999.

Note: You cannot claim exemption from withholding if (1) your income exceeds $700 and includes unearned income (e.g., interest and dividends) and (2) another person can claim you as a dependent on their tax return.

Basic instructions. If you are not exempt, complete the Personal Allowances Worksheet. The worksheets on page 2 adjust your

withholding allowances based on itemized deductions, adjustments to income, or two-earner/two-job situations. Complete all worksheets that apply. They will help you figure the number of withholding allowances you are entitled to claim. However, you may claim fewer allowances.

New—Child tax and higher education credits. For details on adjusting withholding for these and other credits, see Pub. 919, Is My Withholding Correct for 1998?

Head of household. Generally, you may claim head of household filing status on your tax return only if you are unmarried and pay more than 50% of the costs of keeping up a home for yourself and your dependent(s) or other qualifying individuals.

Nonwage income. If you have a large amount of nonwage income, such as interest or dividends, you should consider making estimated tax payments using Form 1040-ES. Otherwise, you may owe additional tax.

Two earners/two jobs. If you have a working spouse or more than one job, figure the total number of allowances you are entitled to claim on all jobs using worksheets from only one W-4. Your withholding will usually be most accurate when all allowances are claimed on the W-4 filed for the highest paying job and zero allowances are claimed for the others.

Check your withholding. After your W-4 takes effect, use Pub. 919 to see how the dollar amount you are having withheld compares to your estimated total annual tax. Get Pub. 919 especially if you used the Two-Earner/Two-Job Worksheet and your earnings exceed $150,000 (Single) or $200,000 (Married). To order Pub. 919, call 1-800-829-3676. Check your telephone directory for the IRS assistance number for further help.

Sign this form. Form W-4 is not valid unless you sign it.

Personal Allowances Worksheet

A Enter "1" for **yourself** if no one else can claim you as a dependent . . . . **A** _____

B Enter "1" if: { • You are single and have only one job; or
• You are married, have only one job, and your spouse does not work; or
• Your wages from a second job or your spouse's wages (or the total of both) are $1,000 or less. } . . **B** _____

C Enter "1" for your **spouse.** But, you may choose to enter -0- if you are married and have either a working spouse or more than one job. (This may help you avoid having too little tax withheld.) . . . . **C** _____

D Enter number of **dependents** (other than your spouse or yourself) you will claim on your tax return. . . **D** _____

E Enter "1" if you will file as **head of household** on your tax return (see conditions under **Head of household** above) . **E** _____

F Enter "1" if you have at least $1,500 of **child or dependent care expenses** for which you plan to claim a credit . . **F** _____

G **New—Child Tax Credit:** • If your total income will be between $16,500 and $47,000 ($21,000 and $60,000 if married), enter "1" for each eligible child. • If your total income will be between $47,000 and $80,000 ($60,000 and $115,000 if married), enter "1" if you have two or three eligible children, or enter "2" if you have four or more . . . . **G** _____

H Add lines A through G and enter total here. Note: This amount may be different from the number of exemptions you claim on your return. ▶ **H** _____

For accuracy, complete all worksheets that apply. {
• If you plan to **itemize or claim adjustments to income** and want to reduce your withholding, see the Deductions and Adjustments Worksheet on page 2.
• If you are **single**, have **more than one job**, and your combined earnings from all jobs exceed $32,000 OR if you are **married** and have a **working spouse or more than one job**, and the combined earnings from all jobs exceed $55,000, see the Two-Earner/Two-Job Worksheet on page 2 to avoid having too little tax withheld.
• If **neither** of the above situations applies, **stop here** and enter the number from line H on line 5 of Form W-4 below. }

- - - - - - - - - - **Cut here and give the certificate to your employer. Keep the top part for your records.** - - - - - - - - - -

Form **W-4**
Department of the Treasury
Internal Revenue Service

Employee's Withholding Allowance Certificate
▶ For Privacy Act and Paperwork Reduction Act Notice, see page 2.

OMB No. 1545-0010
1998

1 Type or print your first name and middle initial | Last name | **2** Your social security number

Home address (number and street or rural route)

City or town, state, and ZIP code

3 ☐ Single ☐ Married ☐ Married, but withhold at higher Single rate.
Note: If married, but legally separated, or spouse is a nonresident alien, check the Single box.

4 If your last name differs from that on your social security card, check here and call 1-800-772-1213 for a new card . . . . . . ▶ ☐

5 Total number of allowances you are claiming (from line H above or from the worksheets on page 2 if they apply) . | **5**

6 Additional amount, if any, you want withheld from each paycheck. . . . . | **6** S

7 I claim exemption from withholding for 1998, and I certify that I meet BOTH of the following conditions for exemption:
• Last year I had a right to a refund of ALL Federal income tax withheld because I had NO tax liability AND
• This year I expect a refund of ALL Federal income tax withheld because I expect to have NO tax liability.
If you meet both conditions, enter "EXEMPT" here. . . . . ▶ | **7**

Under penalties of perjury, I certify that I am entitled to the number of withholding allowances claimed on this certificate or entitled to claim exempt status.

Employee's signature ▶ | **Date** ▶ | , 19

8 Employer's name and address (Employer: Complete 8 and 10 only if sending to the IRS) | **9** Office code (optional) | **10** Employer identification number

Cat. No. 10220Q

Teaching Consumer Concepts

Form D—Personnel Manager/Employee Data Sheet form

Employee Data Sheet

Name_____ Social Security # _____

Address _____ Date of Birth _____ Age _____

City, State, Zip _____ Phone #_____

Marital Status: _____ Single _____ Married _____ Divorced _____ Widowed

Spouse's Name _____

Number of Dependents _____

Pets: _____ Cat _____ Dog _____ None

Number of Miles Driven to Work (one way) _____

Dependents

Name	Social Security #	Boy/Girl	Age
_____	_____	_____	_____
_____	_____	_____	_____
_____	_____	_____	_____
_____	_____	_____	_____

In Case of Emergency:_____
                        NAME   PHONE #   RELATIONSHIP

For Office Use Only:

Date Hired _____   **Job Title** _____

Starting Salary _____   **Education** _____

Total Withholding Allowances (W-4) _____

Health Plan (check one): _____ Single _____ Family

Date Training Completed _____   **Trainer** _____

Dates of Follow-up Meetings _____

Comments:

In File: _____ **JOB APPLICATION** _____ **RÉSUMÉ** _____ **COVER LETTER** _____ **W-4**

Teaching Consumer Concepts

Form E—Personnel Manager/Employee Records form

Employee Records
Class Participation
10 Point Maximum Daily

Name _____ Position _____

(Evaluate employee's efficiency, politeness, attitude, cooperation, and effort in performing her or his job.)

Date	Comments	Points Earned

Total:_____

(Total points possible _____)

Teaching Consumer Concepts

Form F—Personnel Manager/Employee Records form

Employee Records
Summary of Days Missed

Name	Date Missed	Reason	Approved

Teaching Consumer Concepts

Service Station Attendant

Job Description: Computes routine costs of operating a vehicle, including gas, oil changes, tune-ups, and tire depreciation. Determines labor charges on repairs by computing hours logged on time card.

Education Requirements: High school diploma; one year of post-secondary education in auto mechanics required, two years preferred.

Benefits: Starting salary—$18,000, with annual reviews. Health insurance coverage provided—individual. Shopping allowance—$1,000 (new employees only). Sick days—two per quarter. Personal days—five per year.

Duties

Complete an Annual Mileage Worksheet (Form A) for Each Customer

1. Get the gas mileage for the customer's car from the Car Dealer's listings.
2. Determine round-trip miles driven to work (listed on the Employee Data Sheet in the Personnel Manager's files). Multiply by 2 to determine round-trip miles; then multiply by 5 (days per week), and by 52 (weeks per year).
3. Determine the miles driven running errands. Assume 30 miles per week for trips to the bank, grocery store, etc., and multiply by 52.
4. Determine miles driven per year for doctor/dentist/optometrist appointments. Assume a round-trip of 20 miles per visit and the following number of appointments: Adults—4 per year; Children—9 per year; Infants—14 per year.
5. Determine miles driven to visit friends and relatives. Assume 45 miles driven per month and multiply by 12 (months per year).
6. Estimate pleasure driving for the year. Choose from between 100 and 1,000 miles for different customers.
7. Total the miles driven for the year. If the total is less than 7,000, use 7,000 for remaining computations.

Complete a Monthly Statement (Form B) for Each Customer

1. Compute the customer's annual gasoline expenditures.
   - Determine the number of gallons the customer uses in a year (Gallons Used = Miles Driven ÷ Gas Mileage). (Round to whole gallon.)

- Gasoline costs $1.15 per gallon. Determine the customer's annual gas expenditures. (Annual Gasoline Cost = Gallons Used × Price Per Gallon). (Round to whole gallon.)

2. Compute the customer's annual expenditures for oil changes. Assume oil is changed every 3,000 miles. Divide the annual mileage by 3,000 to get the number of oil changes per year. Round to the nearest whole number. Unit cost for oil changes (including new filters) is $15. Determine the customer's expenditures (Annual Cost of Oil Changes = Number of Oil Changes × Price of Oil Change + Sales Tax).

3. Enter the cost of tune-ups ($85), 6 percent Sales Tax, and total the two.

4. Compute the cost of depreciation (wear and tear) on tires. Assume that tires last for 50,000 miles and cost $55 apiece new ($220 plus 6 percent sales tax for four). Divide the annual mileage on your customer's car by 50,000 to determine the percentage of tread used. Round to the nearest thousandth. Then compute the following: Tire Depreciation = Percentage of Tread Used × Price (including tax) of New Tires.

5. Determine monthly payment due. Add all annual costs, which include 6 percent sales tax, to determine total annual costs. Divide by 12 to get the monthly payment.

Complete the Accounts Receivable Cards

Create a separate card for each customer.

1. Enter Amount Due: For each customer, enter the amount of the monthly bill.

2. Enter Amount Paid: As you collect each check, enter the amount of the payment and the check number on the appropriate accounts receivable card and compute the new balance.

Enter All Transactions in the Business Checking Ledger

1. Enter deposits daily:
   - Fill out a business checking deposit slip for all checks received that day.
   - Record the total deposit in the checking ledger.
   - Be sure that all checks are endorsed "For deposit only to the account of Gas & Go."
   - Staple deposit slip and checks together and give to Bank Account Manager or leave in deposit drop box.

2. Reimburse Budget Plus, Inc.—Payroll Account:
   - Make out a check for 80 percent of the daily deposit.
   - Enter the check in the checking ledger.
   - Give the check to the Payroll Clerk.

Teaching Consumer Concepts

Form A—Service Station Attendant/Annual Mileage Worksheet form

Gas & Go Service Station
Annual Mileage Worksheet

Name _____ Date _____

Address _____

Phone _____ S.S. # _____

Gas Mileage _____

Show all computations neatly and completely.

Annual Miles Driven to Work: _____

Annual Miles Driven Running Errands: _____

Annual Miles Driven for Medical Appointments: _____

Annual Miles Driven Visiting Family & Friends: _____

Annual Miles Driven for Pleasure/Entertainment: _____

Total Annual Miles Driven (minimum 7,000): _____

Form B—Service Station Attendant/Monthly Statement form

Gas & Go Service Station
Monthly Statement

DESCRIPTION	QUANTITY	UNIT COST	SALES TAX	ANNUAL COST
Gasoline				
Oil Changes				
Tune-up				
Tire Depreciation				
TOTAL				

TOTAL ANNUAL COST: _____

MONTHLY PAYMENT DUE: _____

Teaching Consumer Concepts

Utilities Manager

Job Description: Computes bills for natural gas, electricity, and water consumption; garbage pickup; and sewer and phone service.

Education Requirements: Undergraduate degree in business and one year of on-the-job experience.

Benefits: Starting salary—$28,000, with annual reviews. Health insurance coverage provided—individual. Shopping allowance—$1,000 (new employees only). Sick days—two per quarter. Personal days—five per year.

Duties

Calculate Monthly Utility Expenses (Form A)

Note: For this simulation, all utilities will incur a 6 percent sales tax.

1. Compute natural gas heating bill. Determine amount due for natural gas use based on the size of the customer's apartment (if heat is not included in rent) or house. Gas use is measured in units of 100 cubic feet. For example, 23 CCF means 2,300 cubic feet. City Utilities, Inc., uses an "Even Pay" plan: The cost of heating your home (which is higher during the winter months) is broken into 12 equal monthly payments. Use the chart and rate information below to calculate customers' gas use.

# Bedrooms	CCF—Homes	CCF—Apartments	Rates:
1	34	21	Usage Charge: $0.67 per CCF used
2	49	30	Monthly Service Charge: $5
3	62	37	Sales Tax: 6%
4	72	Not applicable	

Sample computation for a two-bedroom home:
49 CCF × $0.67 = $32.83 Usage Charge
5.00 Service Charge
$37.83 Subtotal
$37.83 × .06 = 2.27 Sales Tax
$40.10 Total Monthly Charge

2. Compute electric bill. Determine amount due for electricity on the basis of the size of the customer's apartment (if electricity is not

included in rent) or house. Electricity use is measured in kilowatt-hours (kWh). A kilowatt is 1000 watts, or the amount of electricity required to burn a 100-watt light bulb for 10 hours. Use the chart and rate information below to calculate customer's electric bills.

# Bedrooms	Kwh—Homes and Apartments	Rates:
1	527	Usage Charge: $0.0691 per kWh used
2	738	Availability Charge: $0.002 per kWh used
3	949	Monthly Service Charge: $2.50 per month
4	1160	Sales Tax: 6%

Sample computation for a three-bedroom home or apartment:
949 kWh × $0.0691 = $65.58 Usage Charge
949 kWh × $0.002 = $ 1.90 Availability Charge
$ 2.50 Service Charge
$69.98 SubTotal
$69.98 × .06 = $ 4.20 Sales Tax
$74.18 Total Monthly Charge

3. Compute the water and sewer bill. Determine the total bill for water and sewer on the basis of household size.
1-person household— $22.00 / month + 6 percent sales tax
2-person household— $28.00 / month + 6 percent sales tax
3-person household— $33.00 / month + 6 percent sales tax
4-person household— $38.00 / month + 6 percent sales tax
5- or more household—$45.00 / month + 6 percent sales tax

4. Compute garbage pickup bill. The fee for this service is $12 per household per month plus 6 percent sales tax.

5. Compute the phone bill. Determine the cost for phone service on the basis of options chosen and the amount of time spent on the phone. Everyone pays the following charges:

Base Rate $10.00/month
Wire Maintenance $ 0.50/month
FCC Line Charge $ 3.50/month
E911 Surcharge $ 1.00/month

Customers may choose these options:

Extra Extensions $ 1.00/extension/month
Touch-Tone Service $ 1.00/month
Call Waiting $ 2.00/month

To determine a household's phone time, cut out the phone use slips on the following page and put them into an envelope. Have one member of each household draw a slip to determine the monthly phone use (in minutes) for each adult in that household. (Note that daytime use on the slips is minimal because customers are at work during these hours. Night rates include weekends and holidays.) Collect the slips one at a time, and calculate the cost of phone service indicated on each slip using the following rates:

Tolls: _____ minutes of daytime calls × $0.21 = $_____
_____ minutes of evening calls × $0.12 = $_____
_____ minutes of night or weekend calls
× $0.09 = $_____

Add the costs of phone time to the required costs and any optional costs on the utilities bill. Add up all phone costs plus 6% sales tax to get the total phone bill amount for the utilities bill. Paste the phone use slip on the bill.

Phone Use Slips*

PHONE USE	PHONE USE	PHONE USE	PHONE USE	PHONE USE	PHONE USE	PHONE USE
Daytime: 10 min	Daytime: 12 min	Daytime: 8 min	Daytime: 0 min	Daytime: 2 min	Daytime: 5 min	Daytime: 8 min
Evening: 25 min	Evening: 27 min	Evening: 20 min	Evening: 15 min	Evening: 26 min	Evening: 32 min	Evening: 29 min
Night: 35 min	Night: 42 min	Night: 24 min	Night: 45 min	Night: 34 min	Night: 60 min	Night: 26 min
PHONE USE	PHONE USE	PHONE USE	PHONE USE	PHONE USE	PHONE USE	PHONE USE
Daytime: 5 min	Daytime: 0 min	Daytime: 7 min	Daytime: 9 min	Daytime: 4 min	Daytime: 1 min	Daytime: 2 min
Evening: 36 min	Evening: 48 min	Evening: 10 min	Evening: 15 min	Evening: 30 min	Evening: 17 min	Evening: 27 min
Night: 33 min	Night: 17 min	Night: 47 min	Night: 26 min	Night: 20 min	Night: 55 min	Night: 46 min
PHONE USE	PHONE USE	PHONE USE	PHONE USE	PHONE USE	PHONE USE	PHONE USE
Daytime: 3 min	Daytime: 4 min	Daytime: 5 min	Daytime: 6 min	Daytime: 3 min	Daytime: 12 min	Daytime: 4 min
Evening: 37 min	Evening: 36 min	Evening: 29 min	Evening: 23 min	Evening: 28 min	Evening: 17 min	Evening: 23 min
Night: 24 min	Night: 14 min	Night: 26 min	Night: 18 min	Night: 15 min	Night: 46 min	Night: 34 min

*If more slips are needed, copy the page or make your own.

Complete the Accounts Receivable Cards

Create a separate card for each customer.

1. Enter Amount Due: For each customer, enter the amount of the monthly bill.
2. Enter Amount Paid: As you collect each check, enter the amount of the payment and the check number on the appropriate accounts receivable card and compute the new balance.

Enter All Transactions in the Business Checking Ledger

1. Enter deposits daily:
   - Fill out a business checking deposit slip for all checks received that day.
   - Record the total deposit in the checking ledger.
   - Be sure that all checks are endorsed "For deposit only to the account of City Utilities, Inc."
   - Staple deposit slip and checks together and give to Bank Account Manager or leave in deposit drop box.
2. Reimburse Budget Plus, Inc.—Payroll Account:
   - Make out a check for 80 percent of the daily deposit.
   - Enter the check in the checking ledger.
   - Give the check to the Payroll Clerk.

Teaching Consumer Concepts

Form A—Utilities Manager/Monthly Utility Expenses form

CITY UTILITIES, INC.
Monthly Utility Expenses

Name _____   Apartment / House

Address _____   # in Household _____

City, State, Zip _____   # Bedrooms _____

Gas: _____ CCF used	$_____ Usage Charge
(estimated)	$_____ Service Charge
	$_____ Subtotal
	$_____ Sales Tax
Even Pay Plan	$_____ **Total Gas Bill**

Electricity: _____ kWh	$_____ Usage Charge
	$_____ Availability Charge
	$_____ Service Charge
	$_____ Subtotal
	$_____ Sales Tax
	$_____ **Total Electric Bill**

Water and Sewer:	$_____ Base Rate
	$_____ Sales Tax
	$_____ **Total Water & Sewer**

Garbage Pickup:	$_____ Flat Fee
	$_____ Sales Tax
	$_____ **Total Garbage Bill**

Telephone Service:	$_____ Base Rate
	$_____ Wire Maintenance
	$_____ FCC Line Charge
Paste Phone Use slip here.	$_____ E911 Surcharge
	$_____ Extra Extensions
	$_____ Touch-Tone Service
	$_____ Call Waiting
_____ Minutes ($0.21)	$_____ Daytime Calls
_____ Minutes ($0.12)	$_____ Evening Calls
_____ Minutes ($0.09)	$_____ Night, Weekend
	$_____ Subtotal
	$_____ Sales Tax
	$_____ **Total Phone Bill**

Monthly Total for All Utilities: $_____

Teaching Consumer Concepts

Assessments

1040A TAX FORM

Students are now ready to file a tax return, using various documents they gathered during the simulation. Copy and distribute the 1040A forms and instructions that follow and walk students through completion of the form. Then collect the completed tax returns. The forms provided here are for 1997. You might want to give students current-year forms and adjust the instructions here to account for any changes. You will need to supply students with the federal tax tables and the earned income credit table.

QUIZZES

Students must complete a quiz during or at the end of the simulation. This assessment helps students consolidate what they've learned and demonstrate their mastery of curriculum goals.

The quizzes are individualized for each job and test students' knowledge of the positions they held during the simulation. Each quiz requires additional forms that you must copy from the job packets and include with the quiz questions. These forms are listed at the beginning of each quiz.

Students can work on the quizzes whenever they are ready to do so. Different jobs are ready for quizzes at different times, and some quizzes take longer to complete than others. Keep quizzes in a classroom folder, on your desk or with the Personnel Manager. Students work on the quiz in class and return it to the folder at the end of the period if they need to work on it more. They hand the completed quiz in to you. Students can close their business while they work on the quiz.

INSTRUCTIONS FOR COMPLETING FORM 1040A

1. **General information.** Fill in. Indicate whether you wish to donate to the presidential election campaign fund.

2. **Filing status.** If you are single with no children, check box 1; single with children, check box 4; married with or without children, check box 2.

3. **Exemptions.** Claim yourself, your spouse if you're married, and any children you have (include each child's name and Social Security number). Answer all questions carefully.

4. **Adjusted gross income.**
   - Line 7: Enter the amount listed in box 1 of your W-2 form. If you are married, combine your income with your spouse's and enter the total.
   - Line 8a: Enter the interest income listed on your 1099 form.
   - Line 8b: The interest earned on some types of savings plans, such as Individual Retirement Accounts, some life insurance policies, and some mutual funds, is not taxable. No such interest was earned in this simulation, so enter "0" here.
   - Lines 9–13: Enter "0."
   - Line 14: Enter the total of Lines 7 and 8a.
   - Line 15: Enter "0."
   - Line 16 will be the same as line 14.

5. **Standard deduction, exemption amount, and taxable income.**
   - Line 18a: Do not check any boxes.
   - Line 18b: Do not check the box because you are filing a joint return.
   - Follow the directions on the form for Lines 17, 19, 20, 21, and 22.

6. **Tax, credits, and payments.**
   - Line 23: To compute, use the amount on line 22 and the Tax Table.
   - Line 24a: If you have children, complete Schedule 2 (Child and Dependent Care Expenses) to determine the amount of credit you receive.
   - Lines 24b and 24c: Enter "0."
   - Lines 24d and 25: Follow the directions on the form.
   - Lines 26 and 27: Enter "0."
   - Line 28: Follow the directions on the form.
   - Line 29a: Enter amount listed in box 2 of your W-2 form.
   - Line 29b: Enter "0."
   - Line 29c: To qualify for the earned income credit, you must be (1) single with no dependents and earning less than $9,770; (2) married with one dependent and earning less than $25,760; or

Teaching Consumer Concepts

(3) married with two or more dependents and earning less than $29,290. If you qualify, fill out Schedule EIC (Earned Income Credit) to determine the amount of your credit. If you do not qualify, enter "0."
- Line 29e: Enter the total of Lines 29a, 29b, and 29c.
7. **Refund or amount you owe.** Complete either lines 30–32 or lines 33–34.
   - Lines 30–32: If the amount of tax withheld from your paycheck plus any earned income credit (Line 29e) was more than you should have paid in, complete lines 30 and 31 to receive your refund.
   - Line 33: If you have not had enough withheld from your paycheck, complete this line and attach a check for the amount due.
8. Sign and date the tax form; check for addition and subtraction errors; and attach a copy of your W-2 form.

Instructions for Completing Schedule 2, Child and Dependent Care Expenses

Name and Social Security number: If you are married, enter the name and Social Security number of the first person listed on the 1040A form.

Part I: Persons or organizations who provided the care.
- Line 1: provider's name and address—Bubba Bear Day Care, 1289 Lion Den Road, Big Bucks, IA 00000. Write "tax-exempt" in the Identifying Number column. Enter amount paid—use the total on your cash flow summary.
- Answer "no" to "Did you receive dependent care benefits?"

Part II: Credit for child and dependent care expenses.
- Lines 2a and 2b: Enter the name and Social Security number of each of your children. (If you have three children, list only two of them.)
- Line 2C: Enter your total year's payments for day care for each of your children.
- Line 3: Enter the total of the amounts in the line 2c column. Note the limitations on the amounts you can enter.
- Line 4: Enter your earned income from box 1 on your W-2 form. If you are married enter the income of the person whose name appears at the top of this form.
- Line 5: If you are married, enter your spouse's earned income. If you are single, enter your earned income again.
- Lines 6 and 7: Follow the directions on the form.

Teaching Consumer Concepts

- Line 8: Use the amount listed on line 7 and the chart to determine what part (percentage) of your expenses is tax-deductible.
- Line 9: Multiply line 6 by the decimal amount on line 8. Enter the answer on line 24a of your 1040A form.

Instructions for Completing Schedule EIC, Earned Income Credit

- Line 1: Enter your children's names. If you have three children, list only two of them.
- Line 3: Do not check the "yes" boxes.
- Line 2, 4, and 5: Enter the information that the form asks for.
- Line 6: Enter 12 months. If you have an infant, enter the age in months.

To compute the amount of credit, complete the Earned Income Worksheet below.

Earned Income Worksheet

1. Enter the amount from box 1 on your W-2 form. _____
2. Find the amount of Line 1 in the EIC table and enter it here. _____
3. Enter your adjusted gross income (line 16 on Form 1040A). _____
4. Is Line 3 above less than $11,950 and do you have at least one child? If yes, your earned income credit is the amount on Line 2. Enter this amount on Line 29c of your Form 1040A. _____
5. Is Line 3 above greater than $11,950, and do you have at least one child? If yes, find the amount of Line 3 on the EIC table, and enter it here and on Line 29c of your Form 1040A. _____

Your earned income credit is either the amount on Line 2 or the amount on Line 5, whichever is lower.

Instructions for Entering Income Tax on Your Cash Flow Summary

- Enter amount due as expense in April. Do not write a check.
  OR
- Enter refund as income in June.

Form
1040A Department of the Treasury—Internal Revenue Service
U.S. Individual Income Tax Return (U) **1997** IRS Use Only—Do not write or staple in this space.

OMB No. 1545-0085

Label (See page 14.) **Use the IRS label.** Otherwise, please print in **ALL CAPITAL LETTERS.**

L A B E L H E R E

Your first name | Init. | Last name

If a joint return, spouse's first name | Init. | Last name

Home address (number and street). If you have a P.O. box, see page 14. | Apt. no.

City, town or post office. If you have a foreign address, see page 14. | State | ZIP code

Your social security number

Spouse's social security number

For Privacy Act and Paperwork Reduction Act Notice, see page 42.

Presidential Election Campaign Fund (See page 14.)

| | Yes | No |
Do you want $3 to go to this fund? . . . .
If a joint return, does your spouse want $3 to go to this fund? . . . .

Note: *Checking "Yes" will not change your tax or reduce your refund.*

1 ☐ Single

2 ☐ Married filing joint return (even if only one had income)

3 ☐ Married filing separate return. Enter spouse's social security number above and full name here. ▶

4 ☐ Head of household (with qualifying person). (See page 15.) If the qualifying person is a child but not your dependent, enter this child's name here. ▶

5 ☐ Qualifying widow(er) with dependent child (year spouse died ▶ 19   ). (See page 16.)

6a ☐ **Yourself.** If your parent (or someone else) can claim you as a dependent on his or her tax return, **do not** check box 6a.

b ☐ **Spouse**

c Dependents. If more than six dependents, see page 16.

(1) First name	Last name	(2) Dependent's social security number	(3) Dependent's relationship to you	(4) No. of months lived in your home in 1997

No. of boxes checked on 6a and 6b ☐

No. of your children on 6c who:
• lived with you ☐
• did not live with you due to divorce or separation (see page 17) ☐

Dependents on 6c not entered above ☐

Add numbers entered in boxes above ☐

d Total number of exemptions claimed . . . . ▶

		Dollars	Cents

7 Wages, salaries, tips, etc. Attach Form(s) W-2. **7**

8a **Taxable** interest income. Attach Schedule 1 if required. **8a**

b **Tax-exempt** interest. DO NOT include on line 8a. **8b**

9 Dividends. Attach Schedule 1 if required. **9**

10a Total IRA distributions. **10a** | 10b Taxable amount (see page 19). **10b**

11a Total pensions and annuities. **11a** | 11b Taxable amount (see page 19). **11b**

12 Unemployment compensation. **12**

13a Social security benefits. **13a** | 13b Taxable amount (see page 21). **13b**

14 Add lines 7 through 13b (far right column). This is your **total income.** ▶ **14**

15 IRA deduction (see page 21). **15**

16 Subtract line 15 from line 14. This is your **adjusted gross income.** If under $29,290 (under $9,770 if a child did not live with you), see the EIC instructions on page 27. ▶ **16**

Attach Copy B of W-2 and 1099-R here. Cat. No. 14059Z **1997 Form 1040A**

Teaching Consumer Concepts

1997 Form 1040A page 2

17	Enter the amount from line 16.	**17**		

18a Check if:
- ☐ **You** were 65 or older ☐ Blind
- ☐ **Spouse** was 65 or older ☐ Blind

Enter number of boxes checked ▶ 18a ☐

b If you are married filing separately and your spouse itemizes deductions, see page 23 and check here . . . . ▶ 18b ☐

19 Enter the **standard deduction** for your filing status. **But see page 24** if you checked any box on line 18a or 18b **OR** someone can claim you as a dependent.
- Single—4,150
- Married filing jointly or Qualifying widow(er)—6,900
- Head of household—6,050
- Married filing separately—3,450

19

20 Subtract line 19 from line 17. If line 19 is more than line 17, enter 0. **20**

21 Multiply $2,650 by the total number of exemptions claimed on line 6d. **21**

22 Subtract line 21 from line 20. If line 21 is more than line 20, enter 0. This is your **taxable income. If you want the IRS to figure your tax, see page 24.** ▶ **22**

23 Find the tax on the amount on line 22 (see page 24). **23**

24a Credit for child and dependent care expenses. Attach Schedule 2. **24a**

b Credit for the elderly or the disabled. Attach Schedule 3. **24b**

c Adoption credit. Attach Form 8839. **24c**

d Add lines 24a, 24b, and 24c. These are your **total credits.** **24d**

25 Subtract line 24d from line 23. If line 24d is more than line 23, enter 0. **25**

26 Advance earned income credit payments from Form(s) W-2. **26**

27 Household employment taxes. Attach Schedule H. **27**

28 Add lines 25, 26, and 27. This is your **total tax.** ▶ **28**

29a Total Federal income tax withheld from Forms W-2 and 1099. **29a**

b 1997 estimated tax payments and amount applied from 1996 return. **29b**

c **Earned income credit.** Attach Schedule EIC if you have a qualifying child. **29c**

d Nontaxable earned income: amount ▶ and type ▶

e Add lines 29a, 29b, and 29c. These are your **total payments.** ▶ **29e**

30 If line 29e is more than line 28, subtract line 28 from line 29e. This is the amount you **overpaid.** **30**

31a Amount of line 30 you want **refunded to you.** If you want it directly deposited, see page 33 and fill in 31b, 31c, and 31d. **31a**

b Routing number

c Type: ☐ Checking ☐ Savings

d Account number

32 Amount of line 30 you want **applied to your 1998 estimated tax.** **32**

33 If line 28 is more than line 29e, subtract line 29e from line 28. This is the **amount you owe.** For details on how to pay, see page 34. **33**

34 Estimated tax penalty (see page 34). **34**

Sign here

Under penalties of perjury, I declare that I have examined this return and accompanying schedules and statements, and to the best of my knowledge and belief, they are true, correct, and accurately list all amounts and sources of income I received during the tax year. Declaration of preparer (other than the taxpayer) is based on all information of which the preparer has any knowledge.

Your signature	Date	Your occupation

Keep a copy of this return for your records.

Spouse's signature. If joint return, BOTH must sign.	Date	Spouse's occupation

Paid preparer's use only

Preparer's signature	Date	Check if self-employed ☐	Preparer's SSN
Firm's name (or yours if self-employed) and address		EIN	
		ZIP code	

✱ Printed on recycled paper

*U.S. Government Printing Office: 1997 — 419-548

Teaching Consumer Concepts

Schedule 2
(Form 1040A)

Department of the Treasury—Internal Revenue Service

Child and Dependent Care Expenses for Form 1040A Filers (0) **1997**

OMB No. 1545-0085

Name(s) shown on Form 1040A: First and initial(s) | Last | Your social security number

Before you begin, you need to understand the following terms. See **Definitions** on page 50.
- Dependent Care Benefits
- Qualifying Person(s)
- Qualified Expenses
- Earned Income

Part I   Persons or Organizations Who Provided the Care—You **must** complete this part.
(If you need more space, use the bottom of page 2.)

(a) Care provider's name	(b) Address (number, street, apt. no., city, state, and ZIP code)	(c) Identifying number (SSN or EIN)	(d) Amount paid (see page 51)

Did you receive **dependent care benefits?**
— No ——▶ Complete only Part II below.
— Yes ——▶ Complete Part III on the back next.

Caution: *If the care was provided in your home, you may owe employment taxes. See the instructions for Form 1040A, line 27, on page 25.*

Part II   Credit for Child and Dependent Care Expenses

2 Information about your **qualifying person(s).** If you have more than two qualifying persons, see page 51.

(a) Qualifying person's name First	Last	(b) Qualifying person's social security number	(c) Qualified expenses you incurred and paid in 1997 for the person listed in column (a)

3 Add the amounts in column (c) of line 2. DO NOT enter more than 2,400 for one qualifying person or 4,800 for two or more persons. If you completed Part III, enter the amount from line 24.   **3**

4 Enter YOUR **earned income.**   **4**

5 If married filing a joint return, enter YOUR SPOUSE'S earned income (if student or disabled, see page 52); **all others,** enter the amount from line 4.   **5**

6 Enter the **smallest** of line 3, 4, or 5.   **6**

7 Enter the amount from Form 1040A, line 17.   **7**

8 Enter on line 8 the decimal amount shown below that applies to the amount on line 7.

If line 7 is— Over	But not over	Decimal amount is	If line 7 is— Over	But not over	Decimal amount is
$0	10,000	.30	$20,000	22,000	.24
10,000	12,000	.29	22,000	24,000	.23
12,000	14,000	.28	24,000	26,000	.22
14,000	16,000	.27	26,000	28,000	.21
16,000	18,000	.26	28,000	No limit	.20
18,000	20,000	.25			

8 ×

9 Multiply **line 6** by the decimal amount on line 8. Enter the result. Then, see page 52 for the amount of credit to enter on Form 1040A, line 24a.   **9**

For Paperwork Reduction Act Notice, see Form 1040A instructions.   Cat. No. 10749I   1997 Schedule 2 (Form 1040A)

  Teaching Consumer Concepts

SCHEDULE EIC	Earned Income Credit	OMB No. 1545-0074

SCHEDULE EIC
(Form 1040A or 1040)

Department of the Treasury
Internal Revenue Service   (U)

Earned Income Credit
(Qualifying Child Information)
▶ **Attach to Form 1040A or 1040.**
▶ **See instructions on back.**

OMB No. 1545-0074

19**97**

Attachment
Sequence No. **43**

Name(s) shown on return: First and initial(s)	Last	Your social security number

Before you begin . . .

- See the instructions for Form 1040A, lines 29c and 29d, or Form 1040, lines 56a and 56b, to find out if you can take this credit.
- If you can take the credit, fill in the Earned Income Credit Worksheet in the Form 1040A or Form 1040 instructions to figure your credit. **But if you want the IRS to figure it for you, see instructions on back.**

Then, you **must** complete and attach Schedule EIC only it you have a qualifying child (see boxes on back).

Information About Your Qualifying Child or Children

If you have more than two qualifying children, you only have to list two to get the maximum credit.

Caution: If you do not attach Schedule EIC and fill in all the lines that apply, it will take us longer to process your return and issue your refund.	**Child 1**		**Child 2**	
	First name	Last name	First name	Last name
1 Child's name				
2 Child's year of birth	19 ☐☐		19 ☐☐	
3 If the child was born **before 1979** AND—				
a was **under age 24** at the end of 1997 **and** a student, check the "Yes" box, **OR** . . .	☐ Yes		☐ Yes	
b was permanently and totally disabled (see back), check the "Yes" box	☐ Yes		☐ Yes	
4 Enter the child's social security number				
5 Child's relationship to you (for example, son, grandchild, etc.) . .				
6 Number of months child lived with you in the United States in 1997 . .	☐☐ months		☐☐ months	

TIP: Do you want the earned income credit added to your take-home pay in 1998? To see if you qualify, get **Form W-5** from your employer or by calling the IRS at 1-800-TAX-FORM (1-800-829-3676).

For Paperwork Reduction Act Notice, see Form 1040A or 1040 instructions.   Cat. No. 15788F   Schedule EIC (Form 1040A or 1040) 1997

Name _____

Date _____

Period _____

AUDITOR

Forms Required:

Food Fair monthly food bill (Form A—Grocery Store Manager)

Payroll Worksheet (Form A—Payroll Clerk)

Statement of Earnings & Deductions/Payroll checks (Forms B and C—Payroll Clerk)

Monthly Utility Expenses (Form A—Utilities Manager)

It is your job to know how to do everyone else's job so that you can audit—or check—their paperwork. Complete the following tasks.

1. Compute a monthly food bill for Reece and Hugh Carroll of 9024 N. Highland, Hamlet, IA 70000; phone (319) 555-7156. Reece is 39 years old and Hugh is 41 years old. They have four children: Nancy—age 15, Fred—age 12, Nick—age 6, and Sally—age 3. They are on the low-cost plan.

2. Judd Welte is a single teacher with no children. His Social Security number is 560-56-0560. Judd earns $26,240 a year and claims two withholding allowances. Compute his gross semimonthly salary and his payroll deductions and issue his first payroll check (check no. 465).

3. Wes and Daphne Taylor live in a one-bedroom apartment located at 670 S. Pennsylvania Avenue, Big Bucks, IA 00000. They pay for all utilities and have one Touch-Tone phone with no call waiting. This month they talked on the phone for 3 minutes during daytime rates and 15 minutes on the weekend. Compute their monthly utilities bill.

CAR DEALER

Forms Required:

Motor Vehicle Purchase Agreement (Form A—Car Dealer)

Damage/Odometer Disclosure Statements (Forms B and C—Car Dealer)

1. Ramona Wherry of 2905 E. Riverview Drive, Big Bucks, IA 00000, is buying a 1999 Jeep Wrangler 4×4 (VIN 749J893GFAS). After negotiating the price of the vehicle, you agree to sell it for 4 percent less than the advertised sale price of $21,995. Fill out a purchase agreement and the disclosure statements, and calculate your commission on the sale. Ramona's birth month is April; her phone number is (319) 555-7912; and her Social Security number is 111-11-3335.

Name _____

Date _____

Period _____

BANK ACCOUNT MANAGER

Forms Required:

Personal Check Register (Form B—Bank Account Manager)
Checking Deposit Ticket (Form D—Bank Account Manager)
Savings Deposit slips (2) (Form E—Bank Account Manager)
Savings Account Statement (Form I—Bank Account Manager)

1. Lorenzo Caveal of 298 15th Street, Dyersville, IA 00001, received a check for $651.82 from working at Budget Plus. He wants to put 10 percent of his earnings into his savings account and the rest into checking. Fill out a checking deposit slip and savings deposit slip. Lorenzo's savings account number is S-1.

2. Kenisha Howell lives at 4378 Dearborn Street, Cascade, IA 00003. She received a check from Tiger Wills for $256.35. She wants to deposit all but $40 into checking. She also has $3.54 in change, a $10 bill, and a $15 check to put into her savings account. Fill out deposit slips.

3. Fill out a savings account summary for Norma Streeper, (310 Pershing Rd., Lost Nation, IA 00004) using the following information: balance last statement—$5,032.60; deposits—4/5 and 4/20, payroll, $75.50 each and 4/15 and 4/25, cash, $35.75 each. Also compute the interest earned.

4. Fill out Lennie Riese's check register using the information below. His beginning balance is $546.98.

Check No.	Date	Description
	6/3/99	$78.50 car insurance premium (automatically deducted from checking account)
310	6/5/99	$11 for gas to Gas & Go
311	6/6/99	$13.55 to City Utilities
	6/10/99	Deposit from Budget Plus for $780.70
	6/14/99	$25 ATM withdrawal
312	6/15/99	$656 rent to Buck's Apartments
313	6/22/99	$78.32 to Food Fair

Quiz

Name _____

Date _____

Period _____

AUDITOR

Forms Required:
> Food Fair monthly food bill (Form A—Grocery Store Manager)
> Payroll Worksheet (Form A—Payroll Clerk)
> Statement of Earnings & Deductions/Payroll checks (Forms B and C—Payroll Clerk)
> Monthly Utility Expenses (Form A—Utilities Manager)

It is your job to know how to do everyone else's job so that you can audit—or check—their paperwork. Complete the following tasks.

1. Compute a monthly food bill for Reece and Hugh Carroll of 9024 N. Highland, Hamlet, IA 70000; phone (319) 555-7156. Reece is 39 years old and Hugh is 41 years old. They have four children: Nancy—age 15, Fred—age 12, Nick—age 6, and Sally—age 3. They are on the low-cost plan.

2. Judd Welte is a single teacher with no children. His Social Security number is 560-56-0560. Judd earns $26,240 a year and claims two withholding allowances. Compute his gross semimonthly salary and his payroll deductions and issue his first payroll check (check no. 465).

3. Wes and Daphne Taylor live in a one-bedroom apartment located at 670 S. Pennsylvania Avenue, Big Bucks, IA 00000. They pay for all utilities and have one Touch-Tone phone with no call waiting. This month they talked on the phone for 3 minutes during daytime rates and 15 minutes on the weekend. Compute their monthly utilities bill.

CAR DEALER

Forms Required:
> Motor Vehicle Purchase Agreement (Form A—Car Dealer)
> Damage/Odometer Disclosure Statements (Forms B and C—Car Dealer)

1. Ramona Wherry of 2905 E. Riverview Drive, Big Bucks, IA 00000, is buying a 1999 Jeep Wrangler 4×4 (VIN 749J893GFAS). After negotiating the price of the vehicle, you agree to sell it for 4 percent less than the advertised sale price of $21,995. Fill out a purchase agreement and the disclosure statements, and calculate your commission on the sale. Ramona's birth month is April; her phone number is (319) 555-7912; and her Social Security number is 111-11-3335.

Quiz

Name _____

Date _____

Period _____

BANK ACCOUNT MANAGER

Forms Required:

Personal Check Register (Form B—Bank Account Manager)
Checking Deposit Ticket (Form D—Bank Account Manager)
Savings Deposit slips (2) (Form E—Bank Account Manager)
Savings Account Statement (Form I—Bank Account Manager)

1. Lorenzo Caveal of 298 15th Street, Dyersville, IA 00001, received a check for $651.82 from working at Budget Plus. He wants to put 10 percent of his earnings into his savings account and the rest into checking. Fill out a checking deposit slip and savings deposit slip. Lorenzo's savings account number is S-1.

2. Kenisha Howell lives at 4378 Dearborn Street, Cascade, IA 00003. She received a check from Tiger Wills for $256.35. She wants to deposit all but $40 into checking. She also has $3.54 in change, a $10 bill, and a $15 check to put into her savings account. Fill out deposit slips.

3. Fill out a savings account summary for Norma Streeper, (310 Pershing Rd., Lost Nation, IA 00004) using the following information: balance last statement—$5,032.60; deposits—4/5 and 4/20, payroll, $75.50 each and 4/15 and 4/25, cash, $35.75 each. Also compute the interest earned.

4. Fill out Lennie Riese's check register using the information below. His beginning balance is $546.98.

Check No.	Date	Description
	6/3/99	$78.50 car insurance premium (automatically deducted from checking account)
310	6/5/99	$11 for gas to Gas & Go
311	6/6/99	$13.55 to City Utilities
	6/10/99	Deposit from Budget Plus for $780.70
	6/14/99	$25 ATM withdrawal
312	6/15/99	$656 rent to Buck's Apartments
313	6/22/99	$78.32 to Food Fair

Quiz

Name _____

Date _____

Period _____

CHILD CARE WORKER

Forms Required:
> Bubba Bear Day Care rate sheet
> Bubba Bear Day Care Invoices (3) (Form A—Child Care Worker)

1. Jami Jones has an infant (Tavielle) and a three-year-old (Deon). She works days in a bakery and earns $15,500 per year. Her husband works nights in a factory and earns $25,000. Jami needs day care from 8 A.M. to 12 P.M. Complete an invoice for the first month of day care for the two children. Jami lives at 420 N. Cathery Drive, Freedom, IA 56106. Her phone number is (512) 555-4366.

2. Casey Kimball needs day care for her infant daughter (Chelsey) and three-year-old son (Adam) full time while she is at work. She earns $18,000 as an X-ray technician. She is a single mother struggling to make ends meet. Casey lives at 560 N. Ridge Road, Gunther, IA 40000. Her phone number is (512) 555-9843. Complete an invoice for the monthly cost of her children attending Bubba Bear.

COUNTY TREASURER

Forms Required:
> Ward County Car Registration bill (Form A—County Treasurer)
> Ward County Real Estate Tax bill (Form B—County Treasurer)

1. Juan Ellis lives at 432 E. Anamosa Street, Canton, IA 40930. His Social Security number is 389-00-0000 and his birthday is in June. His phone number is (319) 555-2893. He has purchased a 1996 Chevy Cavalier. Use the Car Dealer's listings to complete an auto registration bill for Juan.

2. Leigh Kramer has just purchased a new house located at 234 Brad Street, Big Bucks, IA 00000, as her primary residence. Her phone number is (319) 555-2930, and her Social Security number is 000-58-4444. The home was listed at $69,900. Complete a real estate tax bill for Leigh. (See the house listings on page 76 for any information you need to complete the form.)

Quiz

Name _____

Date _____

Period _____

DEPARTMENT STORE MANAGER

Forms Required:

Heart & Home Sales Invoice (2) (Form A—Department Store Manager)

Heart & Home Credit Card Purchases Statement (Form C—Department Store Manager)

1. Josef and Bettina White want to purchase a table and chairs. They have budgeted about $800 for this. They also need three toys for a four-year-old girl that are educational and build imagination. Complete an invoice for these items and compute your commission. The White family lives at 5389 S. 2nd Street, Big Bucks, IA 00000. Commission Earned: _____

2. Red Benton is looking for a white self-cleaning oven for his kitchen and a small tent for backpacking trips. Red lives at 532 N. Prairie Road, Big Bucks. Fill out an invoice for these items and compute your commission. Commission Earned: _____

3. Harriet Stein of 2304 Luger Lane, Big Bucks, was recently promoted to product manager. She needs a new wardrobe for her job and appliances for her house. Harriet spends $2,850 on these purchases, using her $1,000 shopping allowance and paying an additional $250 by check. She puts the balance of the bill on her credit card. Complete a Credit Card Purchases Statement for Harriet.

GROCERY STORE MANAGER

Forms Required:

Food Fair monthly food bill (2) (Form A—Grocery Manager)

1. Compute a monthly food bill for Tiffany Bettner, a 21-year-old single female who lives alone at 500 W. 7th Avenue, Gladstone, IA 80000. Her phone number is (319) 555-2813. She uses the moderate plan.

2. Compute a monthly food bill for Reece and Hugh Carroll of 9024 N. Highland, Hamlet, IA 70000. Their phone number is (319) 555-7156. Reece is 39 years old and Hugh is 41 years old. They have four children: Nancy—age 15, Fred—age 12, Nick—age 6, and Sally—age 3. They use the low-cost plan.

Quiz

Name _____

Date _____

Period _____

HOUSING COORDINATOR

Forms Required:

House listings (Real Estate Agent's information)

Residential Real Estate Purchase Agreement (Form A—Real Estate Agent)

Financing Worksheet (Form B—Real Estate Agent)

Just 4 You Realty Statement of Account (Form C—Real Estate Agent)

Apartment Lease Agreement (Form D—Leasing Agent)

Deposit Summary/Receipt (Form E—Leasing Agent)

1. Josie Francis and her husband Orlando Kyle want to purchase a two-bedroom house priced between $70,000 and $80,000. They would like the house to have a large lot. Use the following information to complete the tasks listed below: Josie's annual income is $28,000; Orlando's is $25,500. They do not negotiate; they pay the full list price for the house. The purchase agreement is completed on April 5, 1998. Closing date is May 1. Josie's Social Security number is 000-21-5430; Orlando's Social Security number is 034-51-2000. The address of the new home is 673 Franklin, Oxford Mills, IA 88654; the purchase price is $79,900.

   a. Find a home in the real estate listings that meets Josie and Orlando's needs and complete a Purchase Agreement, Financing Worksheet, and Statement of Account. Determine whether an 8 percent interest rate or a 7 percent rate plus 2 points would be the best for them. Assume that they want a 20-year repayment schedule.

   b. Determine how much money they would save in total payments if they chose the same interest rate but paid off the loan in 15 years.

2. Raul Vans is looking for a two-bedroom apartment. He has found what he wants, with a garage for his vehicle, a nonsmoking building, and a yard for his young son to play in. Complete an Apartment Lease Agreement and Deposit Summary/Receipt for Raul. Raul's new address will be 1412 N. Appletree, Big Bucks, IA 00000. His monthly rent is $575. He signs the lease and pays the total deposit and first month's rent on May 7, 1998 (Check # 1105). He can move in on June 1, 1998.

Quiz

Name _____

Date _____

Period _____

INSURANCE AGENT—HOME

Forms Required:

Home Owner/Renter Insurance Application (2) (Form A—Home Insurance Agent)

1. Complete a Home Owner Insurance Application for Kyle A. Jensen, who recently purchased a home for $75,000. His home loan is from Hawkeye Bank and Trust. This home will be his primary residence and is well protected with smoke alarms. He wants the replacement cost endorsement on his contents and answers all Dwelling Information questions "no." Use the following additional information to complete the application: His phone number is (319) 555-3478. The address of the new home is 4590 E. 32nd Avenue, Cadbury, IA 57782. Kyle chooses a $250 deductible. The protection class is 10; and the date of application/effective date is 5/7/98.

LOAN OFFICER

Forms Required:

Car Loan Application (Form A—Loan Officer)

1. Teresa Valdez is planning to buy a 1997 Mercury Tracer, VIN 12GU196K755. She wants to borrow $9,600 of the total purchase price of $12,000. She will also have to pay $630 in sales tax and a $50 title fee. Her trade-in allowance is $1,500. Assume she wants to borrow the full amount the bank will allow.

   • Fill out the table below to see what Teresa's monthly payments would be.

Amount of Loan	Length of Loan	Monthly Payment	Total Monthly Payments
	3 yr.		
	4 yr.		

   • Fill out a car Loan Application for Teresa. She has chosen to pay the loan off in three years. Denise lives at 574 W. 13th Ave., Balwin, IA 50021. Her phone number is (512) 488-2834, and her Social Security number is 485-37-9987.

Quiz

Name _____

Date _____

Period _____

PAYROLL CLERK

Forms Required:
Payroll Worksheet (2) (Form A—Payroll Clerk)
Statement of Earnings & Deductions/Payroll checks (Forms B and C—Payroll Clerk)

1. Judd Welte (Social Security number 560-56-0560) is a single teacher with no children. Judd earns $26,240 a year and claims two withholding allowances. Compute Judd's gross semimonthly salary and payroll deductions, and issue his first payroll check (check no. 465).

2. Lashonda Meyers (Social Security number 389-56-9398) is an insurance agent whose pay is based on salary plus commission. Lashonda is a single mother and claims four withholding allowances. She is on the family health insurance plan. Lashonda's address is 1573 S. Lincoln Way, DeWitt, IA 89264.
   a. Lashonda's first check is based on a guaranteed minimum salary of $750 per month. Complete the first semimonthly check portion of the payroll worksheet.
   b. In addition, Lashonda receives 15 percent commission on her total monthly sales. Compute her commission if she had $7,580 in insurance premiums for the month, and complete the second semimonthly portion of the payroll worksheet.

PERSONNEL MANAGER

Forms Required:
Form W-4: Employee's Withholding Allowance (2) (Form C—Personnel Manager)

1. Fill out a W-4 for Wesley Potter, a single father of two. His children live with him and their grandmother baby-sits them, so Wesley has no day-care costs. Wesley lives at 1286 Washington Drive, Cascade, IA 34875. His Social Security number is 000-11-2222. Wesley paid $1,530 in federal taxes last year.

2. Jessica McDonnell is a loan officer and mother of three. Her husband works part-time (earning $7,000 per year) and takes care of the house and children the rest of the time. Jessica lives at 3586 Asbury Lane, Miles, IA 34875. Her Social Security number is 987-54-3210. Jessica paid $535 in federal income taxes last year. Complete a W-4 for Jessica. How many allowances should Jessica's husband claim on the W-4 for his job? _____

Name _____

Date _____

Period _____

SERVICE STATION ATTENDANT

Forms Required:
Annual Mileage Worksheet (Form A—Service Station Attendant)
Monthly Statement (Form B—Service Station Attendant)

1. Nicki Babcock lives alone at 2387 Hudson Boulevard, Lawrence, IA 39849. Her phone number is (319) 555-2768; her Social Security number is 234-85-8579. Nicki owns a 1991 Dodge Dakota that gets 17 miles per gallon. She drives 15 miles one way to work each day, 20 miles each week running errands, and 250 miles each month visiting friends and family. She drives approximately 1,500 miles a year for pleasure, plus 80 miles a year for medical appointments. Complete the Annual Mileage Worksheet and the Monthly Statement.

UTILITIES MANAGER

Forms Required:
Monthly Utility Expenses (Form A—Utilities Manager)

1. Andre and Carol Petersen live with their two small children in a three-bedroom home at 4521 W. Oak Street, Big Bucks, IA 00000. They have one phone in the kitchen and one in the bedroom. They have Touch-Tone dialing and call-waiting service. Andre and Carol spent 23 minutes on the phone during the day, 15 minutes during the evening, and 37 minutes during the weekend this month. Compute their monthly utilities bill.
2. Wes and Daphne Taylor live in a one-bedroom apartment at 670 S. Pennsylvania Avenue, Big Bucks, IA 00000. They pay for all their utilities and have just one rotary-dial phone with no extra services. This month they talked on the phone for 3 minutes on a weekday and 15 minutes on the weekend. Compute their monthly phone bill.

Auditor's Quiz

1.

Food Fair, Inc.

Billing for the Month of ___Current month___

Name ___Reece and Hugh Carroll___   Phone ___(319) 555-7156___

Address ___9024 N. Highland___

City, State, Zip: ___Hamlet, IA 70000___

Food Plan ___low cost___   Number in Household ___6___

Name	M/F	Age	Base Cost	+/− Percent	Adjusted Cost
Reece	F	39	$125.10	−5%	$118.85
Hugh	M	41	141.20	−5%	134.14
Nancy	F	15	118.80	−5%	112.86
Fred	M	12	137.10	−5%	130.25
Nick	M	6	106.60	−5%	101.27
Sally	F	3	80.20	−5%	76.19

Total Monthly Food Bill: $ ___$673.56___

2. Deductions will vary, depending on tax tables used.

Payroll Worksheet

Employee ___Judd A. Welte___   Occupation ___Teacher___

1st Semimonthly check		2nd Semimonthly check	
Salary	$26,240	Commission Rate	--
Marital status	single	Number of allowances	2
Gross pay	$ 1,093.33	Gross pay/Commission	$
Health insurance deduction	-0-	Health insurance deduction	
Taxable pay	1,093.33	Taxable pay	
Federal withholding	115.00	Federal withholding	
State withholding	47.88	State withholding	
Social Security (FICA)	67.79	Social Security (FICA)	
Medicare	15.85	Medicare	
Net pay	846.81	Net pay	

Budget Plus, Inc.

Employee ___Judd A. Welte___

Statement of Earnings & Deductions

	Current	Year to Date
Gross pay/commission	$1,093.33	$1,093.33
Health insurance withholding	-0-	-0-
Taxable income	1,093.33	1,093.33
Federal tax withholding		
State tax withholding		
FICA		
Medicare		
Net pay		

Pay period ___1___
SS # ___560-56-0560___
Marital status ___S___
Allowances ___2___
Check date ___Today's Date___
Check number ___465___

Budget Plus, Inc.
430 Consumer Lane
Big Bucks, IA 00000

Check No. ___465___

Date ___Today's Date___

Pay to the
Order of ___Judd A. Welte___ -------------------------------- $ _____

_____ Dollars

Big Bucks
Savings Bank

Your Student
Budget Plus, Inc., Payroll Clerk

⑈07L458⑈ L384720⑊ 2428

3.

CITY UTILITIES, INC.
Monthly Utility Expenses

Name ___Wes and Daphne Taylor___   (Apartment) / House

Address ___670 S. Pennsylvania___   # in Household ___2___

City, State, Zip ___Big Bucks, IA 00000___   # Bedrooms ___1___

Gas: ___21___ CCF used (estimated)	$ 14.07	Usage Charge
	$ 5.00	Service Charge
	$ 19.07	Subtotal
	$ 1.14	Sales Tax
Even Pay Plan	$ 20.21	Total Gas Bill
Electricity: ___527___ kWh	$ 36.42	Usage Charge
	$ 1.05	Availability Charge
	$ 2.50	Service Charge
	$ 39.97	Subtotal
	$ 2.40	Sales Tax
	$ 42.39	Total Electric Bill
Water and Sewer:	$ 28.00	Base Rate
	$ 1.68	Sales Tax
	$ 29.68	Total Water & Sewer
Garbage Pickup:	$ 12.00	Flat Fee
	$ 0.72	Sales Tax
	$ 12.72	Total Garbage Bill
Telephone Service:	$ 10.00	Base Rate
	$ 0.50	Wire Maintenance
	$ 3.50	FCC Line Charge
	$ 1.00	E911 Charge
	$ ---	Extra Extensions
	$ 1.00	Touch-Tone Service
	$ ---	Call Waiting
___3___ Minutes ($0.21)	$ 0.63	Daytime Calls
___-0-___ Minutes ($0.12)	$ ---	Evening Calls
___15___ Minutes ($0.09)	$ 1.35	Night, Weekend
	$ 17.98	Subtotal
	$ 1.08	Sales Tax
	$ 19.06	Total Phone Bill

Monthly Total for All Utilities: $ ___123.98___

Bank Account Manager's Quiz

1.

Checking Deposit Ticket

Name ___Lorenzo Caveal___
(Personal account)

Business Name _____

(Business account)
Address ___298 15th Street___
___Dyersville, IA 00001___

Account No. _____

Date ___Today's Date___

sign here for cash received
Big Bucks Savings Bank

Currency		
Coin		
Checks (list each check separately)		
Budget Plus	651	82
Less Savings	65	18
Total	586	64
Less Cash Received		
Net Deposit	586	64

Be sure each item is properly endorsed!

Savings

Withdrawal

Date ___Today's Date___ , 19___
Name ___Lorenzo Caveal___
Address ___298 15th Street___
___Dyersville, IA 00001___
Account number ___S-1___
Amount withdrawn $ _____
Sign here _____

Big Bucks Savings Bank

Deposit

Cash		
Check Description		
From Checking		
Deposit	65	18
Total Checks		
Less Cash Received		
Total Deposit	65	18

2.

Checking Deposit Ticket

Name _____ Kenisha Howell _____
(Personal account)
Business Name _____ 4378 Dearborn St. _____
_____ Cascade, IA 00003 _____
(Business account)
Address _____
_____
Account No. _____
Date _____ Today's Date _____

sign here for cash received

Big Bucks
Savings Bank

Currency		
Coin		
Checks (list each check separately)		
Tiger Wills	256	35
Total	256	35
Less Cash Received	40	00
Net Deposit	216	35

Be sure each item is properly endorsed!

Withdrawal — Savings — Deposit

Date _____ Today's Date _____ , 19 _____
Name _____ Kenisha Howell _____
Address _____ 4378 Dearborn St. _____
_____ Cascade, IA 00003 _____
Account number _____
Amount withdrawn $ _____
Sign here _____

Big Bucks
Savings Bank

Deposit		
Cash	13	54
Check Description		
Tiger Wills	15	00
Total Checks		
Less Cash Received		
Total Deposit	28	54

3.

Savings Account Statement

Name _____ Norma Streeper _____
Address _____ 310 Pershing Rd. _____
City, State, Zip _____ Lost Nation, IA 00004 _____

Big Bucks
Savings Bank
"The Friendly Bank"

Statement summary for savings account # _____ 5-23 _____

Balance last statement: $ 5,032.60

Date	Description	Withdrawal	Deposit	Interest	Balance
4/5	Payroll Deposit		75.50		$5,108.10
4/15	Cash Deposit		35.75		5,143.85
4/20	Payroll Deposit		75.50		5,219.35
4/25	Cash Deposit		35.75		5,255.10

To compute average daily balance:

Day	Date	Balance	Day	Date	Balance	Day	Date	Balance
1	4/1	5,032.60	11	4/11	5,108.10	21	4/21	5,219.35
2	4/2	5,032.60	12	4/12	5,108.10	22	4/22	5,219.35
3	4/3	5,032.60	13	4/13	5,108.10	23	4/23	5,219.35
4	4/4	5,032.60	14	4/14	5,108.10	24	4/24	5,219.35
5	4/5	5,108.10	15	4/15	5,143.85	25	4/25	5,255.10
6	4/6	5,108.10	16	4/16	5,143.85	26	4/26	5,255.10
7	4/7	5,108.10	17	4/17	5,143.85	27	4/27	5,255.10
8	4/8	5,108.10	18	4/18	5,143.85	28	4/28	5,255.10
9	4/9	5,108.10	19	4/19	5,143.85	29	4/29	5,255.10
10	4/10	5,108.10	20	4/20	5,219.35	30	4/30	5,255.10
						31		

$154,558.00 ÷ 30 = $5,151.93
Sum of Daily Balance — **Number of days** — **Average Daily Balance**

Interest Computation:
p Average daily balance: 5,151.93
r Interest rate: 3.5%
t Compounded monthly: 1/12
I Interest Earned; $p \times r \times t$ 15.03 Current Balance $ 5,270.13

4.

Check Register

Personal Check Register Business Checking Ledger for _____ Lenny Riese _____

Check No.	Date	Description of Transaction	Payment/Debit	Deposit/Credit	Balance
		Beginning Balance			546.98
	6/3	Car Deduction - Car Insurance	78.50		468.48
310	6/5	Gas & Go	11.00		457.48
311	6/6	City Utilities	13.55		443.93
	6/10	Deposit - Budget Plus		780.70	1,224.63
	6/14	ATM Withdrawal	25.00		1,199.63
312	6/15	Buck's Apartments	656.00		1,043.63
313	6/22	Food Fair	78.32		965.31
		Service Charge	5.30		960.01

Car Dealer's Quiz

1.

Motor Vehicle Purchase Agreement

Date _____ Today's Date _____ Salesperson _____ Your Student _____
Buyer _____ Ramona Wherry _____ Buyer's Birth Month _____ April _____
Co-buyer _____ Phone Number _____ (319) 555-7912 _____
Address _____ 2905 E. Riverview Drive, Big Bucks, IA 00000 _____

Description of Vehicle Purchased _____ x _____ New _____ Used
Year _____ 1999 _____ Make _____ Jeep _____ Model _____ Wrangler _____
Body Type: ___ Car ___ Pickup ___ Van _x_ Other VIN _____ 749J893GFAS _____
(Vehicle Identification Number)

Down Payment Computation
Purchase Price $21,115.20
Minimum Down Payment: Purchase Price × 20% 4,223.04
Trade-in Allowance **$1,500.00**
Additional Cash Down Payment Required
If trade-in allowance is less than minimum down payment, enter the difference; otherwise enter "0." 2,723.04

Cash Balance Computations
Purchase Price 21,115.20
Subtract: Trade-in Allowance **$1,500.00**
Taxable Amount 19,615.20
Add: Sales Tax (6%) 1,176.91
Title Fee: 15.00
Total Cash Price 20,807.11
Subtract: Additional Cash Down Payment 2,723.04
Cash Balance Due on Delivery 18,084.07

Buyer's Trade-in Certification:
1. The vehicle was never salvaged or rebuilt.
2. The odometer reading is accurate and correct to the best of my knowledge.
3. The following are all in good working condition and meet the manufacturer's specifications: emission control system, engine, transmission, head, block, power train, and frame.
4. Any claims I have made as to the condition of this vehicle are true and correct.
x _____ Ramona Wherry _____

Warranties: I understand that the vehicle I am buying is being sold under the following conditions:
_x_ With a warranty, provided by the manufacturer. The car dealership is not a party to this warranty.
___ As is, with no warranty either implied or expressed.
x _____

This contract is for educational purposes only. It represents the complete agreement regardless of any previous agreements, either oral or written. I certify that I am at least 18 years of age, that I have read this contract and voluntarily agree to its terms.
_____ Ramona Wherry _____ Buyer's Signature _____ 111-11-3335 _____ SS#
_____ Co-buyer's Signature _____ SS#
Accepted by: _____ Your Student _____ Date _____ Today's Date _____
an authorized Colden's Cool Cars Representative

Damage Disclosure Statement

I _____ Your Student _____ (Colden's Cool Cars Dealer) certify the following damage disclosure statement is true and correct.
Year: _____ 1998 _____ Make: _____ Jeep _____ Model: _____ Wrangler _____
VIN: _____ 749J893GFAS _____

1. This motor vehicle has sustained damage of $3,000 or more.
___ yes _x_ no If yes, amount of damage: _____

2. I am aware that this motor vehicle was salvaged or rebuilt.
___ yes _x_ no If yes, ___ salvaged ___ rebuilt ___ previous state where titled

x _____ Your Student _____ _____ Today's Date _____
_____ Authorized Colden's Cool Cars Dealer _____ Date
x _____ Ramona Wherry _____ _____ Today's Date _____
_____ Buyer's Signature _____ Date

Odometer Disclosure Statement

Year: _____ 1998 _____ Make: _____ Jeep _____ Model: _____ Wrangler _____
VIN: _____ 749J893GFAS _____

The odometer currently reads _____ 500 _____.

_x_ This reflects the actual mileage of the vehicle, to the best of my knowledge.

___ Warning: The odometer reading has been tampered with or for some other reason does not reflect the actual mileage of the vehicle.

x _____ Your Student _____ _____ Today's Date _____
_____ Authorized Colden's Cool Cars Dealer _____ Date
x _____ Ramona Wherry _____ _____ Today's Date _____
_____ Buyer's Signature _____ Date

Child Care Worker's Quiz

1.
BUBBA BEAR DAY CARE
Invoice

Account Name ___Jami Jones___   Phone Number ___(512) 555-4366___

Address ___420 N. Cathery Drive, Freedom, IA 56106___

Child	Age	Daily Rate	. Monthly Rate
Deon	3	9.90	214.50
Tavielle	Infant	8.00	173.33

LAUNDRY FEES (Plan A only) ___6.00___

TOTAL DUE ___$393.83___

If you have questions regarding this billing, contact our office. There is a $15 fee for returned checks. Households making less than $20,000 may be eligible for reduced rates. Contact the office for more information.

2.
BUBBA BEAR DAY CARE
Invoice

Account Name ___Casey Kimball___   Phone Number ___(512) 555-9843___

Address ___560 N. Ridge Road, Gunther, IA 40000___

Child	Age	Daily Rate	Monthly Rate
Adam	3	12.75	276.25
Chelsey	Infant	11.05	239.42

LAUNDRY FEES (Plan A only) _____

TOTAL DUE ___$515.67___

If you have questions regarding this billing, contact our office. There is a $15 fee for returned checks. Households making less than $20,000 may be eligible for reduced rates. Contact the office for more information.

County Treasurer's Quiz

1.
Ward County Treasurer's Office
_____Your Student_____, Treasurer

Big Bucks, Iowa

Owner:

Name ___Juan Ellis___ SS# ___389-00-0000___ Birth Month ___June___

Address ___432 E. Anamosa Street___ Phone # ___(319) 555-2893___

City, State, Zip ___Canton, IA 40930___

Car Registration:

Year ___1996___ Make ___Chevy___ Model ___Cavalier___

Body Type Car _x_ Pickup ___ Van ___ VIN ___435J74F43C97___

List Price ___$9,600___ Weight ___2,500___ Age in Years ___2___

Percent of List Price ___100%___ Percent of Weight ___40%___

Pay this amount → Annual Registration Fee: $ ___106.00___

Due in your birth month.   *Make checks payable to Ward County Treasurer*

2.
Ward County Treasurer's Office
_____Your Student_____, Treasurer

Big Bucks, Iowa

HOME OWNER

Name: ___Leigh Kramer___   Homestead Exemption: (Y) or N

Address: ___234 Brad Street___   Phone #: ___(319) 555-2930___

City, State, Zip: ___Big Bucks, IA 00000___   SS#: ___000-58-4444___

RESIDENCE

Address: ___Lot 14 Brad Street___

Market Value: ___$69,900___

TAX COMPUTATION

Rate of Assessment: ___85___ %   Assessed Value: $ ___59,415___

Tax Rate: ___19.5___ mills/$ Annual Taxes Due: $ ___1,159___

Semiannual Payments Due in March & September $ ___579.50___

Department Store Manager's Quiz

1 & 2. There is no Answer Key for problems 1 & 2. Answers depend on what catalog your student uses.

3.
♥ Heart & Home Department Store ♥
Statement of Credit Card Purchases

Buyer's Name: ___Harriet Stein___   Date: ___Today's Date___
Address: ___2304 Luger Lane, Big Bucks, IA 00000___
Salesperson: ___Your Student___   Invoice Number: _____

Total Purchases	$	$2,850.00
Less shopping allowance	$	1,000.00
Amount paid today	$	250.00
Unpaid balance billed to credit card	$	1,600.00
Interest rate:		1.5% per month*
Minimum monthly payment (due the 15th of every month)	$	57.84

*18% annual percentage rate   *Thank you for your business!!*

Grocery Store Manager's Quiz

1.
Food Fair, Inc.

Billing for the Month of ___Current Month___

Name ___Tiffany Bettner___   Phone ___(319) 555-2813___

Address ___500 W. 7th Avenue___

City, State, Zip: ___Gladstone, IA 80000___

Food Plan ___moderate___   Number in Household ___1___

Name	M/F	Age	Base Cost	+/– Percent	Adjusted Cost
Tiffany	F	21	$152.70	+20%	$183.24

Total Monthly Food Bill: $ ___183.24___

2.
Food Fair, Inc.

Billing for the Month of ___Current Month___

Name ___Reece and Hugh Carroll___   Phone ___(319) 555-7156___

Address ___9024 N. Highland___

City, State, Zip: ___Hamlet, IA 70000___

Food Plan ___low cost___   Number in Household ___6___

Name	M/F	Age	Base Cost	+/– Percent	Adjusted Cost
Reece	F	39	$125.10	–5%	$118.85
Hugh	M	41	141.20	–5%	134.14
Nancy	F	15	118.80	–5%	112.86
Fred	M	12	137.10	–5%	130.25
Nick	M	6	106.60	–5%	101.27
Sally	F	3	80.20	–5%	76.19

Total Monthly Food Bill: $ ___673.56___

Housing Coordinator's Quiz

1.

Just 4 You Realty
Residential Real Estate Purchase Agreement

1. On this ___5___ day of ___April___, 1998 at ___1:00___ A.M./P.M. Just 4 You Realty (seller) agrees to sell and convey to ___Josie Francis and Orlando Kyle___ (buyer) the following property located at ___673 Franklin, Oxford Mills, IA 88654___ in Ward County, Iowa, including all fixtures such as lighting, heating, plumbing, outdoor plantings, window covering and hardware, central air-conditioning units and ducting, attached awnings, antennas, attached mirrors, built-in kitchen appliances, wall-to-wall carpeting, water softener, mailbox, storm windows and doors, garage-door openers, and --------------

2. The buyer agrees to pay the seller the sum of $__79,900__ as follows: $__1,500__ will accompany this offer as earnest money to be held by Just 4 You Realty pending final approval of all conditions and terms by both parties. The Balance of $__78,400__ will be paid by cashier's check to Just 4 You Trust Fund and delivered to seller at closing.

3. This offer is made subject to buyer obtaining financing. The buyer shall make application for financing within __5__ business days of the date of this agreement. Written confirmation of approved financing will be made on or before ___April 12, 1998___.

4. Possession and closing date shall be on or before ___May 1, 1998___.

5. The seller will maintain insurance on the described property in the amount of $__79,900__ until the date of closing, at which time the buyer will become responsible for insurance on the property.

6. All real estate taxes shall be prorated between the buyer and the seller as of the date of closing. The seller will pay any expenses necessary to provide merchantable title, free and clear of encumbrances such as back taxes, liens, and assessments unless otherwise noted and agreed upon. The buyer's expenses shall include any loan fees, surveying costs, abstract recording fees, and credit searches. Seller agrees to maintain premises in present condition with the exception of normal wear and tear. Termite inspection shall be the expense of the seller, if required by the buyer's lending institution. It shall be the seller's responsibility and expense to terminate the lease of any existing tenants.

7. Signature of Seller

Name	___Your Student___ Just 4 You Realty	Signature of Buyer Name ___Josie Francis___
Date	___Today's Date___	S.S. # ___000-21-5430___
		Name ___Orlando Kyle___
		S.S. # ___084-51-2000___
		Date ___Today's Date___

Just 4 You Realty
Financing Worksheet

	8%	7%
1. Purchase Price	$79,900.00	$79,900.00
2. Down Payment (10% of Purchase Price)	7,990.00	7,990.00
3. Amount Financed	71,910.00	71,910.00
4. Amount of 2 Points		1,438.00
5.		

PAYMENT CHART

	8%			7%		
	15 years	20 years	30 years	15 years	20 years	30 years
Number of Payments	180	240	360	180	240	360
Monthly Payment	$ 687.21	$ 601.49	$ 527.65	$ 646.35	$ 557.52	$ 478.42
Total Monthly Payments	123,697.21	144,356.53	189,954.73	116,342.49	133,803.68	172,230.35
Total Interest Paid	51,787.21	72,446.53	118,044.73	44,432.49	61,893.68	100,320.35
Down Payment	7,990.00	7,990.00	7,990.00	7,990.00	7,990.00	7,990.00
Points	---	---	---	1,438.20	1,438.20	1,438.20
TOTAL AMOUNT PAID	131,687.21	152,346.53	197,944.73	125,770.69	143,231.88	181,658.55

6. Financing Available:
   Annual Income $ 53,500.00
   Monthly Income $ 4,458.33
   25% of Monthly Income $ 1,114.58
8. Date Loan Approved

7. Payment Schedule Chosen:
   Rate ___7%___
   Years to Repay ___20___
   Monthly Payment $ ___557.52___
   Commission Earned $ ___4,794.00___

Just 4 You Realty
Statement of Account

Date ___Today's Date___

Name	___Josie Francis and Orlando Kyle___ (Buyer)
Property Address	___673 Franklin, Oxford Mills, IA 88654___
# Bedrooms __3__ # Baths __2__ Date of Closing	5/1/98

Real Property Costs:	Amount	Date paid
Purchase price	$79,900	
Earnest money	1,500	
Balance due on purchase price	78,400	
Down payment (less earnest money)	6,490	
Amount financed	71,910	
Other closing costs:		
Appraisal	250	
Abstract of title	125	
Lawyer's opinion	300	
Total Due		

1a. Better option: *7% + 2 pts*

1b.
```
   143,232.80
 − 125,771.00
   $17,461.80
```

2.

Budget Plus Development Corp.
Apartment Lease Agreement

1. On this ___7th___ day of ___May___, ___1998___, Budget Plus Development Corp. (Lessor) and ___Raul Vans___ (Lessee) enter into this monthly rental agreement.

2. Budget Plus Development Corp. agrees to lease the apartment located at ___1412 N. Appletree, Big Bucks, IA 00000___ to the lessee for the purposes of a primary residence.

3. This will be a tenancy from month to month, commencing on the ___1st___ day of ___June___, ___1998___.

4. In return, the lessee agrees to pay consideration of $___$575___ per month, payable in advance but due no later than the ___1st___ of each month.

5. Conditions:
   a. The agreed-upon premises shall be occupied by no more than ___1___ adults and children.
   b. Pets are/are not allowed on the premises.
   c. Utilities will be the responsibility of the lessee, except for ___---___, which shall be paid for by Budget Plus Development Corp.
   d. Lessee shall be responsible for any damage caused by family or guests' negligence.
   e. Lessee shall keep and maintain the premises in a clean and sanitary condition. A security deposit of one month's rent shall be kept until termination of the lease. At that time, an inspection of the premises will be conducted and deductions will be made for damage beyond normal wear and tear. Any remaining security deposit will be returned to the lessee within a period of three (3) weeks.
   f. Lawn care and snow removal shall be the responsibility of Budget Plus Development Corp.
   g. Subletting is not permitted without the prior written consent of the lessor.
   h. Termination of the lease will take place after either party gives thirty (30) days notice or in the event of nonpayment of timely rent, not less than three (3) days after lessee receives written notice of termination of the lease agreement.

6. Signatures:

___Your Student___ Budget Plus Development Corp. Manager	___Raul Vans___ lessee #1
	___May 7, 1998___ date
___date___	lessee #2
	___date___
	lessee #3
	___date___

Budget Plus Development Corp.
Deposit Summary/Receipt

| 1. Tenant's Name | ___Raul Vans___ | Date ___5/7/98___ |
| Address | ___1412 N. Appletree, Big Bucks, IA 00000___ | |

2. Security Deposit	$ ___575.00___
3. Key Deposit	$ ___50.00___
4. Total Deposit	$ ___625.00___
5. 1st Month's Rent	$ ___575.00___
6. Total Due (total deposits + 1st month's rent)	$ ___1,200.00___

7. Date Paid ___5/7/98___ Check Number ___1105___

Approved by ___Your Student___

Home Insurance Agent's Quiz

1.

Home Owner/Renter Insurance Application

Name Kyle A. Jensen	**Date** 5/7/98
Address 4590 E. 32nd Avenue	**Phone** (319) 555-3478
City, State, Zip Cadbury, IA 57782	
Effective Date 5/7/98	**Expiration Date** 5/7/99
Mortgagee Hawkeye Bank & Trust	

Coverage: Check one _X_ HO-3 ____ HO-4
Amounts of Coverage:

A. Dwelling	$75,000	Deductible amount	$250
B. Other structures	7,500	Endorsements:	
C. Personal property	37,500	Replacement cost	X
D. Loss of use	15,000	Waterbed liability	
E. Liability	100,000		
F. Medical Payments	1,000		

Dwelling Information: Check one: _X_ Masonry ____ Frame Protection class: __10__
Smoke alarms on every floor: _X_ Yes ____ No
Check one: _X_ Primary residence ____ Seasonal residence

	Yes	No
1. Any business conducted on premises?		X
2. Any full-time employees of the residence?		X
3. Any swimming pools on premises?		X
If yes, ____ In-ground ____ Aboveground		
4. Any wood/coal-burning stove on premises?		X
5. Any solar heating on premises?		X
6. Any insurance canceled within last three years?		X
If yes, explain below:		

Premiums:

Base premium	$424.00
Discount for higher deductible	63.40
Adjusted base premium	360.40
Optional endorsements:	
Replacement cost	20.00
Waterbed liability	
Total Annual Premium (paid with application)	**$380.40**

Binder of Coverage:
_X_ Coverage is bound as of _____ 5/7/98 _____ (effective date) at _____ A.M./P.M.
Can be canceled by the applicant with written notice or canceled by the company according to the procedures outlined in the policy.
I have read the above application. To the best of my knowledge all statements made are accurate and true.

Applicant's Signature: _Kyle A. Jensen_
Agent's Signature: _Your Student_

Loan Officer's Quiz

1.

Amount of Loan	Length of Loan	Monthly Payment	Total Monthly Payments
9600	3 yr.	305.28	10,989.92
9600	4 yr.	238.90	11,467.20

Big Bucks Savings Bank, Inc.
Big Bucks, IA 00000

Car Loan Application

Buyer Information:	**Co-buyer Information:**
Name Teresa Valdez	**Name**
Address 574 W. 13th Ave.	**Address**
City, State, Zip Baldwin, IA 50021	**City, State, Zip**
Phone (512) 488-2834	**Phone**
SS # 485-37-9987	**SS #**

Vehicle Description: New ____ Used _X_ Year 1998 Make Mercury
Model Tracer Body type car VIN 12CLU196K755

Truth in Lending Disclosures:

Amount Financed	Annual Percentage Rate	Total of Payments	Finance Charge	Total Cost of Vehicle
$9,600	9%	$10,990.08	$1,390.08	$12,380.08

Payment Schedule: Payments start on 8/98 Number of payments 36
Number of years _3_ Amount of monthly payment $305.28
Security: You are giving security in this vehicle as collateral for the loan.
Late Charge: If any payment is not made within 10 days of its due date, a late charge of 5 percent of the amount due or $20.00, whichever is less, will be assessed.
Prepayment: Prepayment is allowed and will decrease the finance charge.

Itemization of Amount Financed:		
A. Total cash price (purchase price & taxes, etc.)		$12,680.00
B. Less amount financed		9,600.00
C. Total down payment		3,080.00
D. Less trade-in allowance		1,500.00
E. Cash balance down		1,580.00

Do not sign this application before you have read it completely. You are entitled to a copy of this paper. You may prepay at any time with no penalty. By signing this paper you are accepting all responsibility for making monthly payments.
Buyer's Signature Teresa Valdez Date 8/10/98
Co-Buyer's Signature _____ Date _____

Payroll Clerk's Quiz

1.

Payroll Worksheet

Employee Judd Welte		Occupation Teacher	
Salary	$1,093.33	Commission Rate	
Marital status single		Number of allowances	2
1st Semimonthly check		**2nd Semimonthly check**	
Gross pay	$ 1,093.33	Gross pay/commission	$
Health insurance deduction		Health insurance deduction	
Taxable pay	1,093.33	Taxable pay	
Federal withholding	115.00	Federal withholding	
State withholding	47.88	State withholding	
Social Security (FICA)	67.79	Social Security (FICA)	
Medicare	15.85	Medicare	
Net pay	846.81	Net pay	

Budget Plus, Inc.   Employee Judd Welte

Statement of Earnings & Deductions

	Current	Year to Date		
Gross pay/commission	1,093.33	1,093.33	Pay period	1
Health insurance withholding	-0-	-0-	SS #	560-56-0560
Taxable income	1,093.33	1,093.33	Marital status	S
Federal tax withholding	115.00	115.00	# Allowances	2
State tax withholding	47.88	47.88	Check date	Today's Date
FICA	67.79	67.79	Check number	465
Medicare	15.85	15.85		
Net pay	846.81	846.81		

Budget Plus, Inc.
430 Consumer Lane
Big Bucks, IA 00000

Check No. 465
Date Today's Date

Pay to the Order of Judd Welte -------- $ 846 81/100
eight hundred forty-six and 81/100 -------- **Dollars**

Big Bucks Savings Bank

Your Student
Budget Plus, Inc., *Payroll Clerk*

⑈071458⑈ ⑈384720⑈ 2428

2.

Payroll Worksheet

Employee Lashonda Meyers		Occupation Insurance Agent	
Salary	$750.00	Commission Rate	15%
Marital status single		Number of allowances	4
1st Semimonthly check		**2nd Semimonthly check**	
Gross pay	$ 750.00	Gross pay/Commission	$ 1,137.00
Health insurance deduction	75.00	Health insurance deduction	75.00
Taxable pay	675.00	Taxable pay	1,062.00
Federal withholding	20.00	Federal withholding	80.00
State withholding	19.85	State withholding	44.99
Social Security (FICA)	46.50	Social Security (FICA)	70.49
Medicare	10.88	Medicare	16.49
Net pay	$577.77	Net pay	$850.03

Personnel Manager's Quiz

1.

Form W-4 (1998)

Purpose. Complete Form W-4 so your employer can withhold the correct Federal income tax from your pay. Because your tax situation may change, you may want to refigure your withholding each year.

Exemption from withholding. If you are exempt, complete only lines 1, 2, 3, 4, and 7, and sign the form to validate it. Your exemption for 1998 expires February 16, 1999.

Note: You cannot claim exemption from withholding if (1) your income exceeds $700 and includes unearned income (e.g., interest and dividends) and (2) another person can claim you as a dependent on their tax return.

Basic instructions. If you are not exempt, complete the Personal Allowances Worksheet. The worksheets on page 2 adjust your

withholding allowances based on itemized deductions, adjustments to income, or two-earner/two-job situations. Complete all worksheets that apply. They will help you figure the number of withholding allowances you are entitled to claim. However, you may claim fewer allowances.

New—Child tax and higher education credits. For details on adjusting withholding for these and other credits, see Pub. 919, Is My Withholding Correct for 1998?

Head of household. Generally, you may claim head of household filing status on your tax return only if you are unmarried and pay more than 50% of the costs of keeping up a home for yourself and your dependent(s) or other qualifying individuals.

Nonwage income. If you have a large amount of nonwage income, such as interest or dividends, you should consider making estimated tax payments using Form 1040-ES. Otherwise, you may owe additional tax.

Two earners/two jobs. If you have a working spouse or more than one job, figure the total number of allowances you are entitled to claim on all jobs using worksheets from only one W-4. Your withholding will usually be most accurate when all allowances are claimed on the W-4 filed for the highest paying job and zero allowances are claimed for the others.

Check your withholding. After your W-4 takes effect, use Pub. 919 to see how the dollar amount you are having withheld compares to your estimated total annual tax. Get Pub. 919 especially if your earnings exceed $150,000 (Single) or $200,000 (Married). To order Pub. 919, call 1-800-829-3676. Check your telephone directory for the IRS assistance number for further help.

Sign this form. Form W-4 is not valid unless you sign it.

Personal Allowances Worksheet

- A. Enter "1" for **yourself** if no one else can claim you as a dependent . . . . **A** 1
- B. Enter "1" if:
  - You are single and have only one job; or
  - You are married, have only one job, and your spouse does not work; or
  - Your wages from a second job or your spouse's wages (or the total of both) are $1,000 or less. } . . . **B** 1
- C. Enter "1" for your **spouse.** But, you may choose to enter -0- if you are married and have either a working spouse or more than one job. (This may help you avoid having too little tax withheld.) . . . . **C**
- D. Enter number of **dependents** (other than your spouse or yourself) you will claim on your tax return . . . . **D** 2
- E. Enter "1" if you will file as **head of household** on your tax return (see conditions under Head of household above) . **E** 1
- F. Enter "1" if you have at least $1,500 of **child or dependent care expenses** for which you plan to claim a credit . . **F**
- G. **New—Child Tax Credit:** • If your total income will be between $16,500 and $47,000 ($21,000 and $60,000 if married), enter "1" for each eligible child. • If your total income will be between $47,000 and $80,000 ($60,000 and $115,000 if married), enter "1" if you have two or three eligible children, or enter "2" if you have four or more . . . . . **G** 5
- H. Add lines A through G and enter total here. **Note:** This amount may be different from the number of exemptions you claim on your return. ▶ **H** 5

For accuracy, complete all worksheets that apply.
- • If you plan to **itemize or claim adjustments to income** and want to reduce your withholding, see the Deductions and Adjustments Worksheet on page 2.
- • If you are **single, have more than one job,** and your combined earnings from all jobs exceed $32,000 OR if you are **married and have a working spouse or more than one job,** and the combined earnings from all jobs exceed $55,000, see the Two-Earner/Two-Job Worksheet on page 2 to avoid having too little tax withheld.
- • If **neither** of the above situations applies, **stop here** and enter the number from line H on line 5 of Form W-4 below.

-------- Cut here and give the certificate to your employer. Keep the top part for your records. --------

Form W-4
Department of the Treasury
Internal Revenue Service

Employee's Withholding Allowance Certificate
▶ For Privacy Act and Paperwork Reduction Act Notice, see page 2.

OMB No. 1545-0010
1998

1. Type or print your first name and middle initial: **Wesley** — Last name **Potter** — 2 Your social security number **000 11 2222**

Home address (number and street or rural route): **1286 Washington Drive**
City or town, state, and ZIP code: **Cascade, IA 34875**

3. ☒ Single ☐ Married ☐ Married, but withhold at higher Single rate. **Note:** If married, but legally separated, or spouse is a nonresident alien, check the Single box.

4. If your last name differs from that on your social security card, check here and call 1-800-772-1213 for a new card ▶ ☐

5. Total number of allowances you are claiming (from line H above or from the worksheets on page 2 if they apply) . **5** 5
6. Additional amount, if any, you want withheld from each paycheck . . . **6** $0
7. I claim exemption from withholding for 1998, and I certify that I meet **BOTH** of the following conditions for exemption:
- • Last year I had a right to a refund of **ALL** Federal income tax withheld because I had **NO** tax liability **AND**
- • This year I expect a refund of **ALL** Federal income tax withheld because I expect to have **NO** tax liability.
If you meet both conditions, enter "EXEMPT" here . . . . . . ▶ **7**

Under penalties of perjury, I certify that I am entitled to the number of withholding allowances claimed on this certificate or entitled to claim exempt status.

Employee's signature ▶ *Wesley Potter* — Date ▶ Today's Date, 19

8. Employer's name and address (Employer: Complete 8 and 10 only if sending to the IRS) | 9 Office code (optional) | 10 Employer identification number

Cat. No. 10220Q

2.

Form W-4 (1998)

Purpose. Complete Form W-4 so your employer can withhold the correct Federal income tax from your pay. Because your tax situation may change, you may want to refigure your withholding each year.

Exemption from withholding. If you are exempt, complete only lines 1, 2, 3, 4, and 7, and sign the form to validate it. Your exemption for 1998 expires February 16, 1999.

Note: You cannot claim exemption from withholding if (1) your income exceeds $700 and includes unearned income (e.g., interest and dividends) and (2) another person can claim you as a dependent on their tax return.

Basic instructions. If you are not exempt, complete the Personal Allowances Worksheet. The worksheets on page 2 adjust your

withholding allowances based on itemized deductions, adjustments to income, or two-earner/two-job situations. Complete all worksheets that apply. They will help you figure the number of withholding allowances you are entitled to claim. However, you may claim fewer allowances.

New—Child tax and higher education credits. For details on adjusting withholding for these and other credits, see Pub. 919, Is My Withholding Correct for 1998?

Head of household. Generally, you may claim head of household filing status on your tax return only if you are unmarried and pay more than 50% of the costs of keeping up a home for yourself and your dependent(s) or other qualifying individuals.

Nonwage income. If you have a large amount of nonwage income, such as interest or dividends, you should consider making estimated tax payments using Form 1040-ES. Otherwise, you may owe additional tax.

Two earners/two jobs. If you have a working spouse or more than one job, figure the total number of allowances you are entitled to claim on all jobs using worksheets from only one W-4. Your withholding will usually be most accurate when all allowances are claimed on the W-4 filed for the highest paying job and zero allowances are claimed for the others.

Check your withholding. After your W-4 takes effect, use Pub. 919 to see how the dollar amount you are having withheld compares to your estimated total annual tax. Get Pub. 919 especially if your earnings exceed $150,000 (Single) or $200,000 (Married). To order Pub. 919, call 1-800-829-3676. Check your telephone directory for the IRS assistance number for further help.

Sign this form. Form W-4 is not valid unless you sign it.

Personal Allowances Worksheet

- A. Enter "1" for **yourself** if no one else can claim you as a dependent . . . . **A** 1
- B. Enter "1" if:
  - You are single and have only one job; or
  - You are married, have only one job, and your spouse does not work; or
  - Your wages from a second job or your spouse's wages (or the total of both) are $1,000 or less. } . . . **B** 0
- C. Enter "1" for your **spouse.** But, you may choose to enter -0- if you are married and have either a working spouse or more than one job. (This may help you avoid having too little tax withheld.) . . . . **C** 0
- D. Enter number of **dependents** (other than your spouse or yourself) you will claim on your tax return . . . . **D** 0
- E. Enter "1" if you will file as **head of household** on your tax return (see conditions under Head of household above) . **E** 0
- F. Enter "1" if you have at least $1,500 of **child or dependent care expenses** for which you plan to claim a credit . . **F** 0
- G. **New—Child Tax Credit:** • If your total income will be between $16,500 and $47,000 ($21,000 and $60,000 if married), enter "1" for each eligible child. • If your total income will be between $47,000 and $80,000 ($60,000 and $115,000 if married), enter "1" if you have two or three eligible children, or enter "2" if you have four or more . . . . . **G** 0
- H. Add lines A through G and enter total here. **Note:** This amount may be different from the number of exemptions you claim on your return. ▶ **H** 4

For accuracy, complete all worksheets that apply.
- • If you plan to **itemize or claim adjustments to income** and want to reduce your withholding, see the Deductions and Adjustments Worksheet on page 2.
- • If you are **single, have more than one job,** and your combined earnings from all jobs exceed $32,000 OR if you are **married and have a working spouse or more than one job,** and the combined earnings from all jobs exceed $55,000, see the Two-Earner/Two-Job Worksheet on page 2 to avoid having too little tax withheld.
- • If **neither** of the above situations applies, **stop here** and enter the number from line H on line 5 of Form W-4 below.

-------- Cut here and give the certificate to your employer. Keep the top part for your records. --------

Form W-4
Department of the Treasury
Internal Revenue Service

Employee's Withholding Allowance Certificate
▶ For Privacy Act and Paperwork Reduction Act Notice, see page 2.

OMB No. 1545-0010
1998

1. Type or print your first name and middle initial: **Jessica** — Last name **McDonnell** — 2 Your social security number **987 54 3210**

Home address (number and street or rural route): **3586 Ashbury Lane**
City or town, state, and ZIP code: **Miles, IA 34875**

3. ☐ Single ☒ Married ☐ Married, but withhold at higher Single rate. **Note:** If married, but legally separated, or spouse is a nonresident alien, check the Single box.

4. If your last name differs from that on your social security card, check here and call 1-800-772-1213 for a new card ▶ ☐

5. Total number of allowances you are claiming (from line H above or from the worksheets on page 2 if they apply) . **5** 4
6. Additional amount, if any, you want withheld from each paycheck . . . **6** $0
7. I claim exemption from withholding for 1998, and I certify that I meet **BOTH** of the following conditions for exemption:
- • Last year I had a right to a refund of **ALL** Federal income tax withheld because I had **NO** tax liability **AND**
- • This year I expect a refund of **ALL** Federal income tax withheld because I expect to have **NO** tax liability.
If you meet both conditions, enter "EXEMPT" here . . . . . . ▶ **7**

Under penalties of perjury, I certify that I am entitled to the number of withholding allowances claimed on this certificate or entitled to claim exempt status.

Employee's signature ▶ *Jessica McDonnell* — Date ▶ Today's Date, 19

8. Employer's name and address (Employer: Complete 8 and 10 only if sending to the IRS) | 9 Office code (optional) | 10 Employer identification number

Cat. No. 10220Q

Service Station Attendant Quiz

1.

Gas & Go Service Station
Annual Mileage Worksheet

Name: Nicki Babcock — Date: Today's Date
Address: 2387 Hudson Boulevard, Lawrence, IA 39849
Phone: (319) 555-2768 — S.S. #: 234-85-8579
Gas Mileage: 17

Show all computations neatly and completely.

Annual Miles Driven to Work:	$15 \times 2 \times 5 \times 52$	7,800
Annual Miles Driven Running Errands:	20×52	1,040
Annual Miles Driven for Medical Appointments:		80
Annual Miles Driven Visiting Family & Friends:	250×12	3,000
Annual Miles Driven for Pleasure/Entertainment:		1,500
Total Annual Miles Driven (minimum 7,000):		13,420

Gas & Go Service Station
Monthly Statement

DESCRIPTION	QUANTITY	UNIT COST	SALES TAX	ANNUAL COST
Gasoline	789 Gal.	$ 1.15		$ 907.35
Oil Changes	4	15.00	$0.90	63.60
Tune-up	1	85.00	5.10	90.10
Tire Depreciation	0.2681	220.00	13.20	62.50
TOTAL			$19.20	$1,123.55

TOTAL ANNUAL COST: $1,123.55
MONTHLY PAYMENT DUE: $ 93.63

Utilities Manager's Quiz

1.
CITY UTILITIES, INC.
Monthly Utility Expenses

Name	Andre and Carol Petersen	Apartment / (House)
Address	4521 W. Oak St.	# in Household ___4___
City, State, Zip	Big Bucks, IA 00000	# Bedrooms ___3___

Gas: __62__ CCF used
(estimated)

$	41.54	Usage Charge
$	5.00	Service Charge
$	46.54	Subtotal
$	2.79	Sales Tax
Even Pay Plan $	49.33	**Total Gas Bill**

Electricity: __949__ kWh

$	65.58	Usage Charge
$	1.90	Availability Charge
$	2.50	Service Charge
$	69.98	Subtotal
$	4.20	Sales Tax
$	74.18	**Total Electric Bill**

Water and Sewer:

$	38.00	Base Rate
$	2.28	Sales Tax
$	40.28	**Total Water & Sewer**

Garbage Pickup:

$	12.00	Flat Fee
$	0.72	Sales Tax
$	12.72	**Total Garbage Bill**

Telephone Service:

		$	10.00	Base Rate
		$	0.50	Wire Maintenance
		$	3.50	FCC Line Charge
		$	1.00	E911 Surcharge
		$	1.00	Extra Extensions
		$	1.00	Touch-Tone Service
		$	2.00	Call Waiting
23 Minutes	($0.21)	$	4.83	Daytime Calls
15 Minutes	($0.12)	$	1.80	Evening Calls
37 Minutes	($0.09)	$	3.33	Night, Weekend
		$	23.96	Subtotal
		$	1.74	Sales Tax
		$	30.70	**Total Phone Bill**

Monthly Total for All Utilities: $ 207.21

2.
CITY UTILITIES, INC.
Monthly Utility Expenses

Name	Wes and Daphne Taylor	(Apartment) / House
Address	670 S. Pennsylvania	# in Household ___2___
City, State, Zip	Big Bucks, IA 00000	# Bedrooms ___1___

Gas: __21__ CCF used
(estimated)

$		Usage Charge
$		Service Charge
$		Subtotal
$		Sales Tax
Even Pay Plan $		**Total Gas Bill**

Electricity: __527__ kWh

$		Usage Charge
$		Availability Charge
$		Service Charge
$		Subtotal
$		Sales Tax
$		**Total Electric Bill**

Water and Sewer:

$		Base Rate
$		Sales Tax
$		**Total Water & Sewer**

Garbage Pickup:

$		Flat Fee
$		Sales Tax
$		**Total Garbage Bill**

Telephone Service:

		$	10.00	Base Rate
		$	0.50	Wire Maintenance
		$	3.50	FCC Line Charge
		$	1.00	E911 Charge
		$	---	Extra Extensions
		$		Touch-Tone Service
		$	---	Call Waiting
3 Minutes	($0.21)	$	0.63	Daytime Calls
-0- Minutes	($0.12)	$	---	Evening Calls
15 Minutes	($0.09)	$	1.35	Night, Weekend
		$	16.98	Subtotal
		$	1.02	Sales Tax
		$	18.00	**Total Phone Bill**

Monthly Total for All Utilities: $ 18.00

We want to hear from you! Your valuable comments and suggestions will help us meet your current and future classroom needs.

Your name_____Date_____

School name_____Phone_____

School address_____

Grade level taught_____Subject area(s) taught_____Average class size_____

Where did you purchase this publication?_____

Was your salesperson knowledgeable about this product?   Yes_____   No_____

What monies were used to purchase this product?

____School supplemental budget   ____Federal/state funding   ____Personal

Please "grade" this Walch publication according to the following criteria:

Quality of service you received when purchasing ....A   B   C   D   F
Ease of use...A   B   C   D   F
Quality of content..A   B   C   D   F
Page layout ....A   B   C   D   F
Organization of material ....A   B   C   D   F
Suitability for grade level...A   B   C   D   F
Instructional value...A   B   C   D   F

COMMENTS:_____

_____

What specific supplemental materials would help you meet your current—or future—instructional needs?

_____

Have you used other Walch publications? If so, which ones?_____

May we use your comments in upcoming communications?   ____Yes   ____No

Please **FAX** this completed form to **207-772-3105,** or mail it to:

Product Development, J. Weston Walch, Publisher, P.O. Box 658, Portland, ME 04104-0658

We will send you a **FREE GIFT** as our way of thanking you for your feedback.   **THANK YOU!**